Writing Essentials for the Beginner Pianist

Building a foundation for piano technique through the discovery of the relationships between scales, chords, and cadences.

For ages 5 and up.

Major and Minor keys Covered:

CCRiddles™
≡Music Theory in Riddle Form≡

ABOUT CATHERINE A. THOMPSON

CATHERINE ANN THOMPSON, B.M., M.A. ET, has a diverse background as a multi-instrumentalist (flute, piano, harp, guitar), freelance musician, educator, and expressive arts therapist in the Los Angeles area. As adjunct faculty at Pasadena City College, she has developed and taught the special grant-funded Music Appreciation program for Older and Disabled Adults at Pasadena City College in Pasadena, CA. She continues to share and perform music as freelance pianist, accompanying instrumentalists and vocalists, and as a church music director. In addition to maintaining a studio of private students, she has performed and collaborated as a pianist with numerous ballet and modern dance companies , chamber ensembles, and soloists in the cities of New Orleans, Boston, Detroit, Toronto Canada, and the former Soviet Union. She is an active member and adjudicator of the MTAC (Music Teachers Association of California), American Federation of Musicians Local 47, and International Association of Expressive Arts Therapists. She has 30+ years experience teaching students of all ages, including students with physical and mental disabilities and autism. She promotes the importance of developing customized formats for teaching according to a student's own learning style. She began her collaboration as a content editor and consultant with Clara Castano and Peter Yazbeck for CCRIDDLES™ products in 2008.

ABOUT CCRIDDLES

CLARA CASTANO is the President and product developer of CCRiddles products. As a result of her teaching expertise with adults and children, she promotes her insights into the benefits of creative drills, learning styles, and memorization techniques. She became inspired to create the CCRiddles™ Learning Cards™ and Music Theory Workbooks during her sixteen years of collaboration with Peter Yazbeck. Their mutual goal to offer a playful and less intimidating method for tutoring basic music theory concepts is now available with CCRiddles' series of Learning Cards™ and test workbooks.

Music and content editor: Catherine A. Thompson
Designer: Clara Castano
Cover artwork: Kenneth Welch
Interior illustrations: Sibelius Software
First printing 2014

ISBN 1-941747-00

TABLE OF CONTENTS

Also from CCRiddles™. . .

Music Theory Prep Level Workbook
Peter Yazbeck and Catherine A. Thompson

Learning Cards™ Prep Level Companion
Clara Castano and Catherine A. Thompson

Music Theory Level 1 Workbook
Peter Yazbeck and Catherine A. Thompson

Learning Cards™ Level 1 Companion
Clara Castano and Catherine A. Thompson

Music Theory Level 2 Workbook
Peter Yazbeck and Catherine A. Thompson

Learning Cards™ Level 2 Companion
Clara Castano and Catherine A. Thompson

Music Theory Level 3 Workbook
Peter Yazbeck and Catherine A. Thompson

Learning Cards™ Level 3 Companion
Clara Castano and Catherine A. Thompson

Music Theory Level 4 Workbook
Peter Yazbeck and Catherine A. Thompson

Learning Cards™ Level 4 Companion
Clara Castano and Catherine A. Thompson

Music Theory Level 5 Workbook
Peter Yazbeck and Catherine A. Thompson

Learning Cards™ Level 5 Companion
Clara Castano and Catherine A. Thompson

Music Theory Level 6 Workbook
Peter Yazbeck and Catherine A. Thompson

Learning Cards™ Level 6 Companion
Clara Castano and Catherine A. Thompson

Music Theory Level 7 Workbook
Peter Yazbeck and Catherine A. Thompson

Learning Cards™ Level 7 Companion
Clara Castano and Catherine A. Thompson

Learning Cards™ Elementary Level 1, 2, & 3
Peter Yazbeck and Clara Castano

Learning Cards™ Secondary Level 1, 2, & 3
Peter Yazbeck and Clara Castano

Learning Cards™ Advanced Level 1, 2, & 3
Peter Yazbeck and Clara Castano

Learning Essentials 1, 2, 3, 4, 5, & 6
Peter Yazbeck and Clara Castano

CCRiddles™
≡Music Theory in Riddle Form≡

P.O. Box 363 · Newbury Park · CA 91319
www.ccriddles.com | 805-338-4170

Introduction to Writing Essentials for the Beginner Pianist

Writing Essentials for the Beginner Pianist is a multi-purpose workbook for early level pianists or any general musician using the keyboard to begin the study of basic scales and triads. Each concept is presented initially, as an activity of discovery and experimentation. The collaboration between the student and teacher will promote the best results by using the element of analysis as a positive factor in these useful presentations of music theory within basic piano patterns. The benefits of this approach save time, as well as support other efforts to simplify music theory and effective practice of piano technique. Developing muscle memory that is supported by visual and cognitive factors will accelerate the student's overall understanding of the essential elements of general musicianship by using this practical and informative book. A technical supplement with fingerings is included for keyboard practice and for use in the lesson assignment as needed.

Writing Essentials for the Beginner Pianist has been created for any age group to do the following:

1. Learn 5-finger patterns built on the major and minor tetrachords, major tonic and dominant triads; be introduced to the parallel and relative minor relationships, as well as learn the (8-note) major and relative natural minor scale patterns, and the major V-I authentic cadence.

2. Be a tool for self-study for independent learners who wish to benefit from the analysis of the piano patterns and their connection to music theory.

3. Be an interactive teaching narrative for non-reading students or young readers.

4. Be an activity oriented step-by-step guide for the individual or for group piano/keyboard activities that are exploring piano patterns related to music theory.

5. Develop early level keyboard technique that does not rely strictly on rote or kinesthetic learning. A helpful glossary is included with helpful definitions related to the exercises.

6. Develop "hand-eye" coordination supported by the cognitive understanding of patterns.

7. Assist in easy memorization of music theory related to piano patterns, scales and chords.

8. Provide mini-theory lessons using activities that can be adapted or presented in any order as part of any lesson plan or pedagogy syllabus.

9. Varied activities and skills to adapt to any pace of learning or style of teaching.

10. Improve awareness of keyboard geography and develop recognition of patterns that support future sight-reading skills and ear-training.

11. Build confidence by using easy-to-follow sequential style practice habits that support organized practice and the ability to follow directions.

12. Grow in awareness of the interconnectedness of all the music elements involved in good technical execution in the performance of repertoire.

HOW TO USE THIS BOOK & TECHNIQUE EXERCISES:

Depending on the needs of the student, there are options for topics to meet the needs of any student's study plan. Some of the material exceeds the preparatory level of expectations, but for ambitious students or older students we included some additional material.

The first two books in the elementary series: *Writing Essentials for the Beginner Pianist* and *Writing Essentials for the Early-Elementary Pianist* are divided basically by tone centers. *The Beginner Pianist* presents the Major keys of: C, G, D, A, E, and F, <u>along with their parallel and natural relative minors.</u> Within each chapter there are 8 worksheets with varied assignments. An adult student may wish to work completely through a chapter, while a teacher with younger age students might wish to teach the major 5-note patterns of each chapter first, followed by the corresponding parallel minor patterns, followed by the simple introduction to the major scale in easy keys (played tetrachord style with the notes split between the two hands…or begin teaching the major scale fingerings hands separately or together).

Depending on the ability and age of the student, this book can be a helpful resource beyond the first year of keyboard study. A technical supplement is included with the corresponding scales and chords that provides the standard fingerings. *The Early-Elementary Pianist* continues further with the remaining major and minor keys in the Circle of Fifths and also provides additional focus on the construction of the authentic V-I (perfect) cadence, the IV-I plagal cadence and the I-V half (imperfect) cadence.

I have witnessed over 30 years, transfer students who play well beyond their actual comprehension of the elements of their repertoire, but falter when performing technical exercises because they have neglected their music theory or have not had a balanced approach in their lessons with corresponding repertoire, technique and music theory presented in a synchronized format. Remarkable results have been achieved with the practice of combining music theory with the exercises and a corresponding music composition. It is so easy to indulge a student who is musical and just wants to play pieces, but it is a disservice to avoid the necessary foundation that ultimately gives them confidence to know what they are doing and to identify the patterns in the music that help them memorize and articulate with ease. It makes sense! This series hopes to fill in that gap or provide a student (or a teacher with such a student), a resource for review or for instruction.

Author & Editor – Catherine A. Thompson

<u>Recommended Music Theory Curriculum</u>:

CCRiddles™ *Learning Cards™ Elementary Level 1, 2, & 3*

CCRiddles™ *Music Theory Prep Level Workbook* and *Prep Level Companion Cards*

CCRiddles™ *Music Theory Level 1 Workbook* and *Level 1 Companion Cards*

Helpful Terms Related to the keyboard

accidental: Any sharps, flats and naturals that raise or lower a note by a half-step.

> **flat** (♭): An accidental that lowers the note by one half-step (down to the next key on piano).

> **natural** (♮): An accidental that cancels the sharp or flat (returns to the original white key).

> **sharp** (♯): An accidental that raises the note by one half-step (up to the next key on piano).

cadence: The chords that end a phrase or section of a composition.

> **authentic cadence**: Cadence using the V̲ chord to the I̲ chord (I̲-V̲-I̲)

half-step: On the keyboard it is the next key to the right or left and it is the key between the whole-step.

hand position: The placement of hands on the keyboard that prepares the pattern of notes to be played. Placing the hands on the tonic and dominant defines the position: C & G = C position.

key signature: At the beginning of a piece (and every staff afterwards) accidentals (sharps or flats) may or may not be included to indicate the main key or tonality of a piece. For pianists, this helps them identify and navigate the hand positions and possible chord patterns related to the main key.

lowercase letters: They are non-capital letters used for identifying non-major scales and chords. Minor scales and chords should always be written with lowercase letters.

major scale: A pattern of notes with the formula: W-W-H +W+ W-W-H.

natural minor scale: A pattern of notes with the formula W-H-W + W-H-W + W.

parallel scales: Scales that have the same tonic and name (ex. C major and c minor), but different key signatures.

pentascale: A five-note scale built on any note.

> **major pentascale**: A five-note scale built with the first 5 notes of a major scale W-W-H + W. The half-step is between the 3rd and 4th notes (or scale degrees).

> **minor pentascale**: A five-note scale built on the first 5 notes of any minor scale W-H-W + W. The half-step is between the 2nd and 3rd notes (or scale degrees).

Helpful Terms Related to the keyboard

relative scales: Scales that have different tonics, but share the same notes and the same key signatures. Example: F major has one flat: B♭. d minor has one flat :B♭.

Roman numerals: Types of numbers used to define chords in music notation. Upper case Roman numerals are topped off and lowercase roman numerals are not. Example: Major authentic cadence is I-V-I and a minor cadence is i-v-i...except when the cadence has a major dominant, then it would be i-V-i.

scale degrees: The numerical reference to each note of the scale. Example: The 1st note is the 1st degree, and the 2nd note is the 2nd degree, etc.

> **dominant**: The 5th scale degree (the 5th note of the scale).

> **tonic**: The 1st scale degree (the 1st note of the scale).

tetrachord: Basically, four tones with various combinations of whole-step and half-step patterns that are the elementary cell structures of scales in Western music. Example: W-W-H (major tetrachord) and W-H-W (minor tetrachord).

uppercase letters: Capital letters. These are used to notate major scales and chords.

whole-step: On the keyboard a whole-step always has a key between the two notes. Example: F to G is a whole-step and the black key (F♯), is the half-step between. B♭ to C is a whole-step and the note B is the half-step between. Two half-steps = a whole-step. The 1st scale degree to the 2nd scale degree is a whole-step. Example: C to D.

_____

_____

_____

_____

_____

_____

_____

_____

Building the 5-Note C Major Scale

Major Tetrachord + Whole-Step
(W - W - H) + (W)

1. Write the **C Major** pentascale (5-note scale) in both clefs and add any accidentals.

2. Using capital (uppercase) letters, write the name of each note on the first line.

3. Mark the half-steps (H) and the whole-steps (W) on the second line.

4. Write the finger-numbers on the third line.

5. Circle the two fingers and note-names with half-steps in each hand, and on the staff.

(Left Hand)

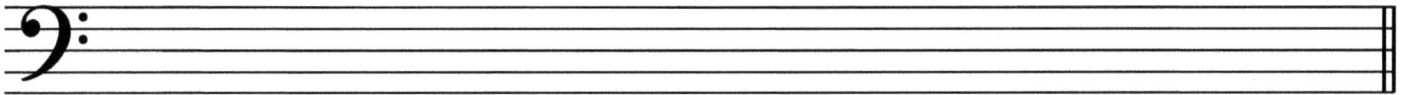

Note-name:

W-H pattern:

Finger-number:

(Right Hand)

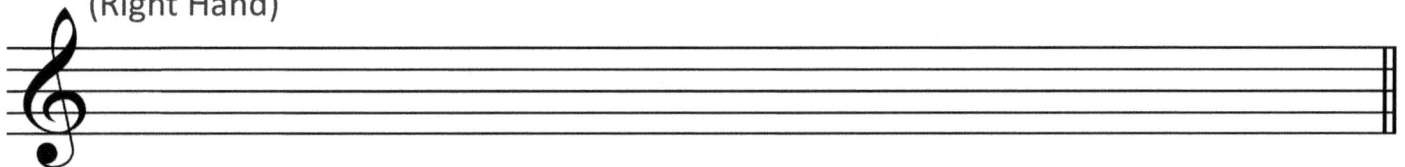

Note-name:

W-H pattern:

Finger-number:

▌▌▌ Keyboard Activities

6. Play a 5-note scale up and down on every note of the **C Major** pentascale.

7. This 5-note scale uses _____ white keys and _____ black keys.

Learning the Middle C and C Major Hand Position

Both thumbs on C

L.H. ————— R.H.

Fingering: 5 4 3 2 1/1 2 3 4 5

Note-Name:

1. Write each note of the **middle C Major** position below the keyboard diagram.

2. Highlight the notes for both hands in middle C position. Circle the half-steps and fingerings in the **middle C Major** position.

3. The L.H. half-steps are _____ and _____. The R.H. half-steps are _____ and _____.

4. What is the bottom note of the left hand? _____

L.H.   R.H.

Scale degree:

5. Color the **C Major** position for both hands.

6. Write and circle the note-names of the 1st, 3rd, and 5th degrees on the keyboard for both hands. This is the **C Major** chord. It starts on ___ and ends on ___.

7. How many white keys are between your two hand positions? _____

8. Notice the difference between the location of **middle C position** and **C position.** How is the left-hand different than the right-hand?

▮▮▮ Keyboard Activities

9. Play a chord on every note of the **C Major** pentascale. What chord is your favorite?

10. How many half-steps between the notes C and E? _____ And between E and G? _____

Major Scale= 2 Major Tetrachords <u>Connected</u> with a Whole-Step

This is how we build it: W-W-H + **W** + W-W-H = major scale

tetrachord   tetrachord

Hint: Be sure to keep a half-step between the 3rd and 4th notes and the 7th and 8th notes.

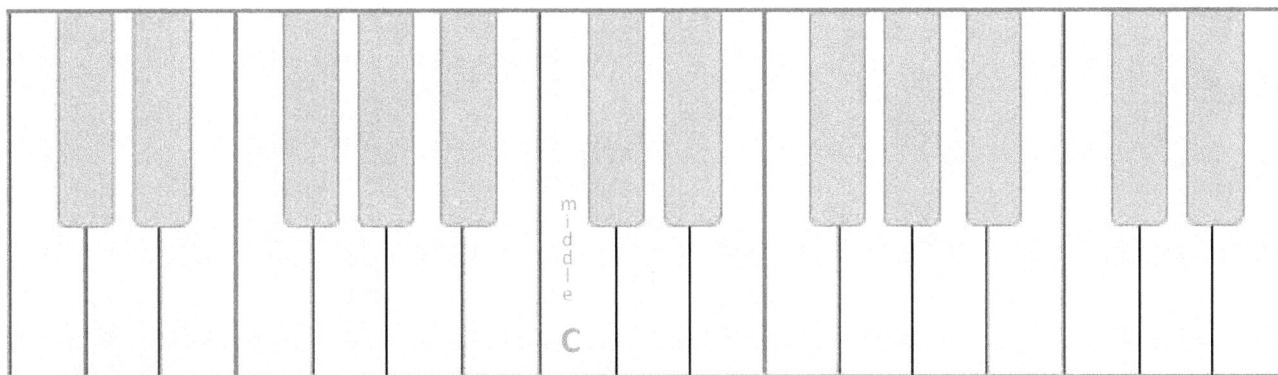

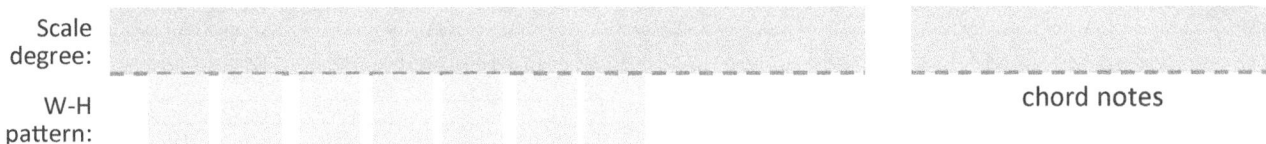

Scale degree:

W-H pattern:

middle C

chord notes

1. Start below middle C. Using the above formula, write each note from **C** to **C**.

2. Write the scale degrees. Identify the whole-steps (W) and the half-steps (H).

3. Color the half-steps in each tetrachord. They are: _____ to_____ and _____ to _____.
   What whole-step connects the two tetrachords?   _____ to _____.

4. Starting on middle C, build a chord by using the 1st, 3rd, and 5th notes of the **C Major** scale. Write and circle the chord notes on the above keyboard.
   The notes of the **C Major** chord are: _____, _____, _____.

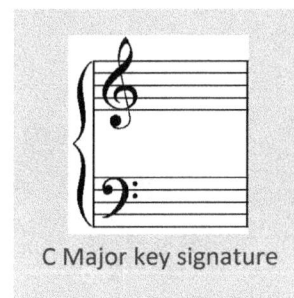

L.H.   R.H.

C Major chords

C Major key signature

5. Write the chords in both clefs. Notice which chord uses line notes and which chord uses space notes.

6. Play and say the **C Major** scale and chord. Notice that it has no ♯s or ♭s, so the key signature is empty. The key signature is the clue for your hand position!

| The chord built on the 1st note of the scale is called the **tonic** chord ($\underline{\text{I}}$) | The chord built on the 5th note of the scale is called the **dominant** chord ($\underline{\text{V}}$) |

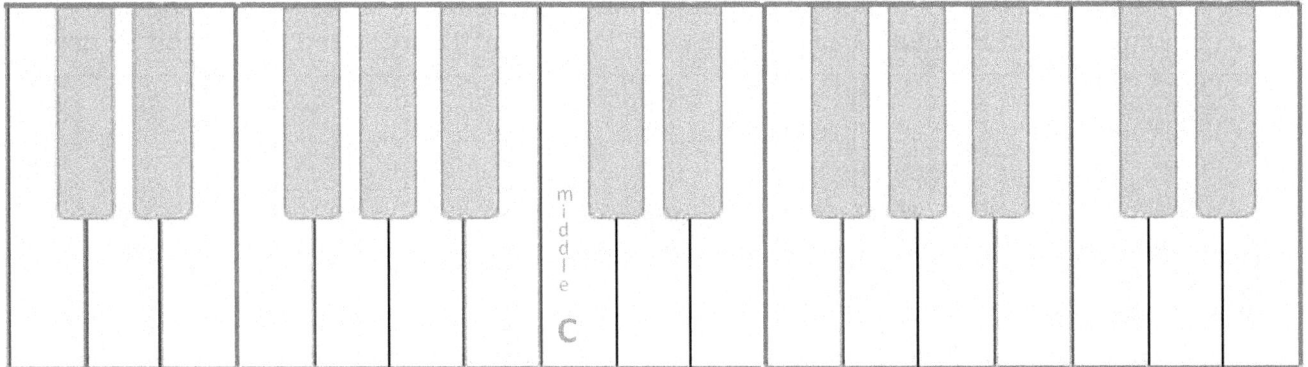

tonic chord + dominant chord + tonic chord = authentic cadence

Chord-name*:

$\underline{\text{I}}$	$\underline{\text{V}}$	$\underline{\text{I}}$	$\underline{\text{I}}$	$\underline{\text{V}}$	$\underline{\text{I}}$
tonic	dominant	tonic	tonic	dominant	tonic

When you write major scales or chords, ALWAYS use capital letters.

▌▌▌▌ Keyboard Activities

1. Write the 5 notes of the **C Major** position for the left hand. Circle the 1st and 5th notes.

2. Play a chord on the 1st note and a chord on the 5th note. Then, write them on the staff above. These are the MOST important chords in the key of **C Major**.

3. Highlight the dominant chord on the keyboard starting on the 5th note of **C Major**

4. The tonic note is _____ and its chord is on the _____ degree of the scale. The dominant note is _____ and its chord is on the _____ degree of the scale.

5. Hands alone, play back and forth between the two chords, then try playing with both hands together.

Building the Parallel C Minor 5-Note Scale

Major: W-W-H - W
major tetrachord

Minor: W-H-W - W
minor tetrachord

The **major** 5-note scale has a half-step between the 3rd and 4th notes.

The **minor** 5-note scale has a half-step between the 2nd and 3rd notes.
(Move your 3rd finger down a half-step)

C Major

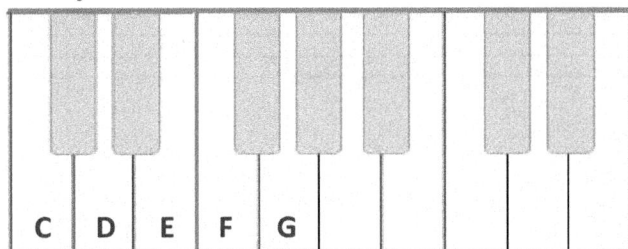

C D E F G

Scale degree:

W or H pattern:

c minor

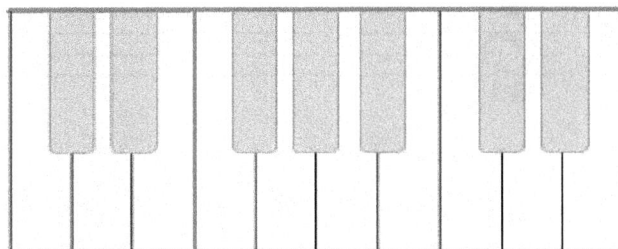

Scale degree:

W or H pattern:

1. On the left keyboard, write the scale degrees and the W-H pattern for the **C Major** 5-note scale.

2. Play the **C Major** pattern, but now lower the 3rd note by a half-step to create a half-step between the 2nd and 3rd notes.

3. What kind of accidental is used? _____ Name the lowered note: _____.

4. Write the new **c minor** 5-note scale on the right keyboard. _____, _____, _____, _____, _____. (*ALWAYS use smaller lowercase letters for minor*).

5. What finger changes position? _____ Mark or color the half-steps on the keyboards above. The half-step in the 5-note **c minor** scale is between the notes _____ and _____. Notice where the half-step is between the major and minor tetrachords and how it changes the 5-note scales.

▐▐▌ Keyboard Activities

6. This minor 5-note scale uses _____ white key(s) and _____ black key(s).

7. Which fingers play the black key in both hands? LH:_____ RH: _____

Building the C Minor Chord

(Left Hand)

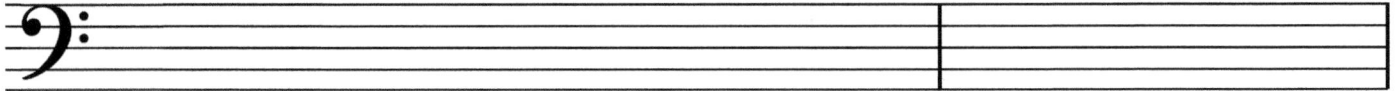

Note-name:

Finger-number:

c minor chord

(Right Hand)

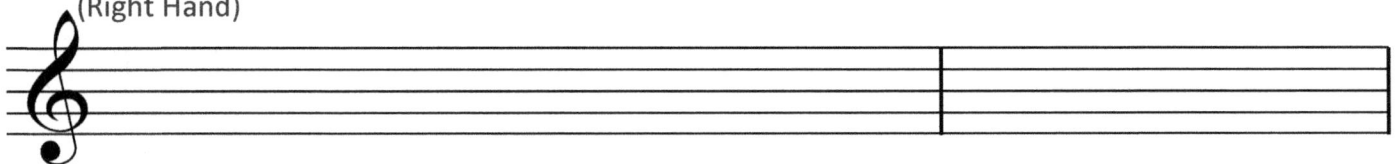

Note-name:

Finger-number:

c minor chord

1. Write the **c minor** pentascale (5-note scale) in both clefs and add any accidentals.

2. Write the note-names and the finger-numbers below the name of the notes.

3. Circle the two fingers and note-names with the half-step in each hand.

4. On the staff, highlight the 1st, 3rd, and 5th notes and write the chord on the staff. The notes of the **c minor** chord are: _____, _____, _____.

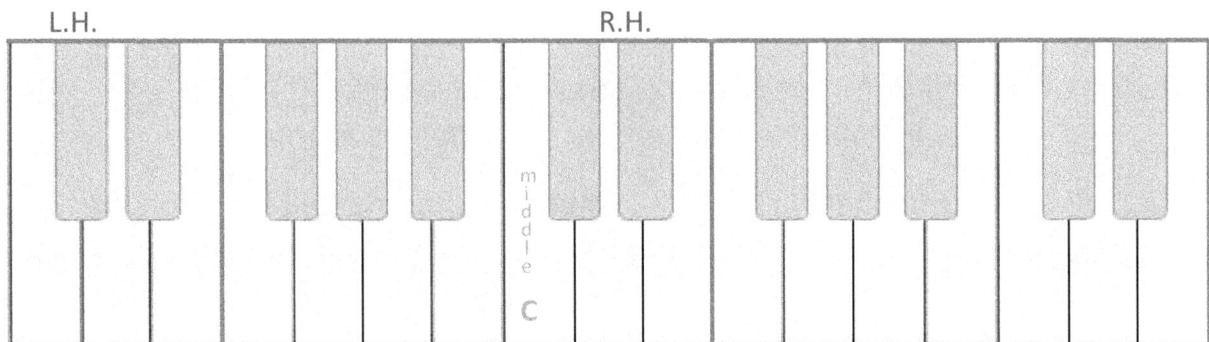

L.H.   R.H.

middle C

5. Write and highlight the notes of the **c minor** chord on the keyboard above.

6. While at your own keyboard, practice switching from **c minor** to **C Major**. Notice how your hand position changes as you move the 3rd finger from the e♭ to the E♮.

C Major's Relative Minor Scale is *A Natural Minor*

How we build it: **W-H-W + W-H-W + W** = natural minor scale

🎹 **Keyboard Activities**

Looking at the **C Major** scale and key signature (see page 3), do the following activities:

1. What is the 6th note of the **C Major** scale? _____. Highlight the note on the left keyboard below.

2. Using the same notes and accidentals, play a scale on the 6th note of the **C Major** scale to make *the relative natural minor scale of C Major*. Notice it uses the same notes and keys as **C Major**, but begins and ends on the note A (the 6th note of **C Major**).

3. The **C Major** and **a minor** scales use _____ white key(s) and _____ black key(s). They are *relative scales* because they share the same notes and use the same key signature.

<u>C</u> Major scale

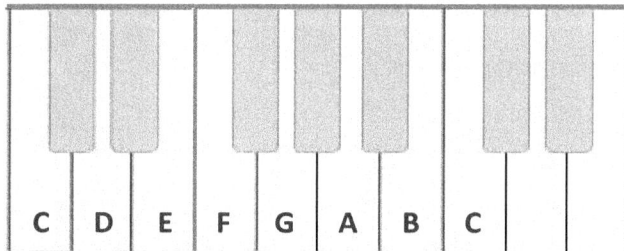

Scale degree:

W-H pattern:

_____ minor scale (highlight the 5-note scale)

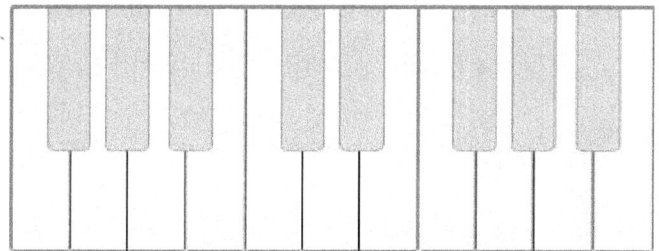

Scale degree:

W-H pattern:

4. Using the same notes as **C Major**, but starting on the note A, write the scale on the keyboard diagram. Highlight the new 5-note **a minor** scale.
   The notes are: _____, _____, _____, _____, _____.

5. Circle the scale degrees and keyboard notes where the half-steps are in both of these relative scales. Notice how they are different. The half-steps in the **a natural minor** scale are between the scale degrees: _____ & _____, and _____ & _____; and between the notes: _____ & _____, and _____ & _____.

Writing and Playing the A Minor Chord

1. Write the **a minor** pentascale (5-note scale) in both clefs and add any accidentals.

2. Write the finger-numbers and note-names below the staff. Circle the 1st, 3rd, and 5th fingerings and note-names in each hand.

3. Circle and highlight the 1st, 3rd, and 5th notes and write the chord on the staff.
The notes of the **a minor** chord are: _____, _____, _____.

(Left Hand)   (Right Hand)

Finger-number: a min chord   a min chord

Note-names:

4. Highlight and write the notes of the **a minor** chord on the keyboard below.

5. How many half-steps are between the note A and the note C? _____

6. How many half-steps are between the note C and the note E? _____

7. What notes are shared in the **C Major** and **a minor** chord? _____ & _____

L.H.   R.H.

middle C

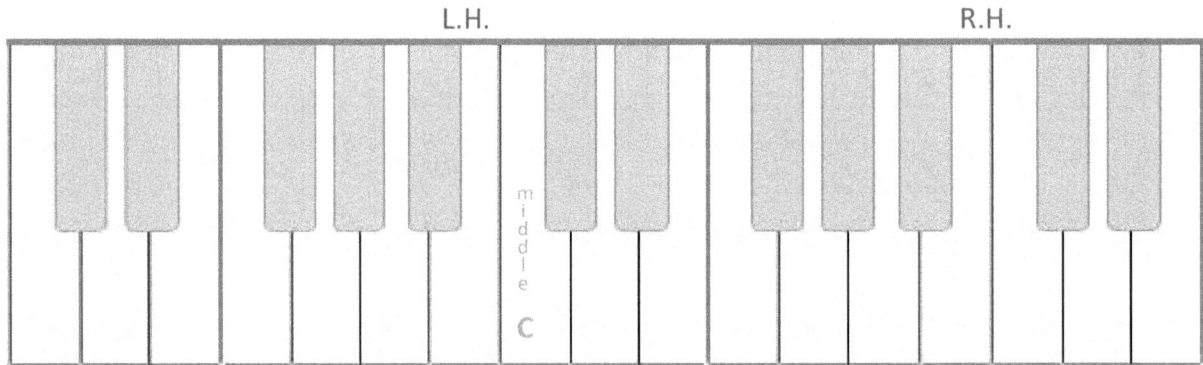

Challenge Activities

Building more chords on the **C Major** scale notes: (Circle the correct answer).

8. Play a chord on the 2nd note of **C Major**. Is it major or minor?

9. Play a chord on the 3rd note of **C Major**. Is it major or minor?

10. Play a chord on the 4th note of **C Major**. Is it major or minor?

11. Play a chord on the 5th note of **C Major**. Is it major or minor?

Major Tetrachord + Whole-Step
(W - W - H) + (W)

1. Write the **G Major** pentascale (5-note scale) in both clefs and add any accidentals. (Write the major note names in capital letters.)

2. Mark the half-steps and the whole-steps on the second line.

3. Write the finger-numbers. Circle the fingerings and note-names with half-steps in each hand, and on the staff.

4. Highlight the 1ˢᵗ, 3ʳᵈ, and 5ᵗʰ notes on each staff.

(Left Hand)

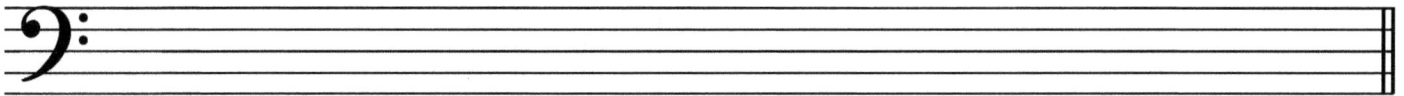

Note-name:

W-H pattern:

Finger-number:

(Right Hand)

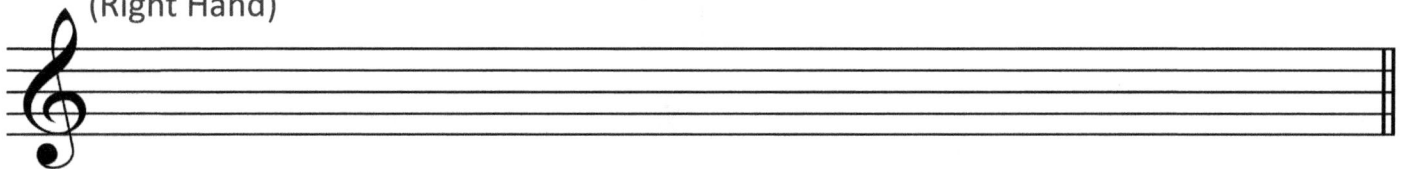

Note-name:

W-H pattern:

Finger-number:

▐▌▌ Keyboard Activities

5. Play your **G Major** 5-note scale up and down using staccato notes.

6. Play your 5-note scale with half notes and then with quarter notes.

7. This 5-note scale uses _____ white keys and _____ black keys.

L.H.   R.H.

middle C

Fingering: 5 4 3 2 1   1 2 3 4 5

Note-Name:

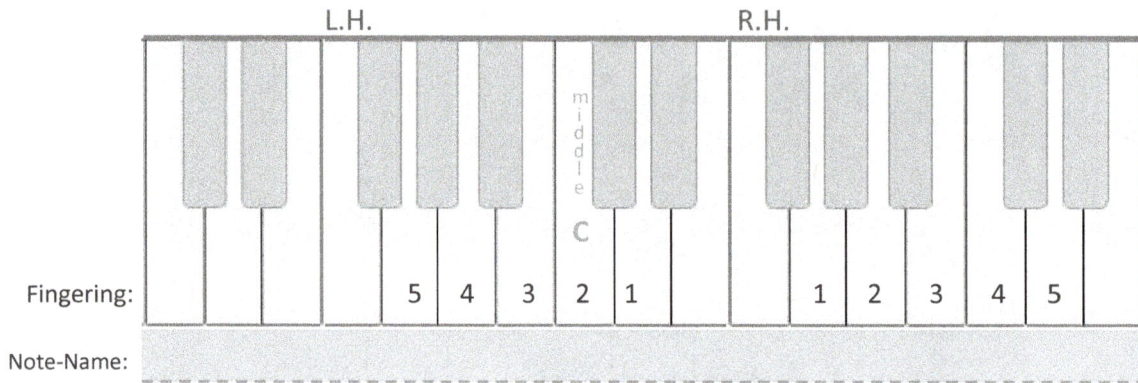

1. Write each note of the **G Major** position on the keyboard diagram.

2. Highlight the **G Major** pentascale above and below middle C.

3. Circle the note-names and fingerings of the half-step in each hand.

4. The half-step is between the notes _____ and _____. This hand position stretches from the notes _____ to _____.

G Position Chords

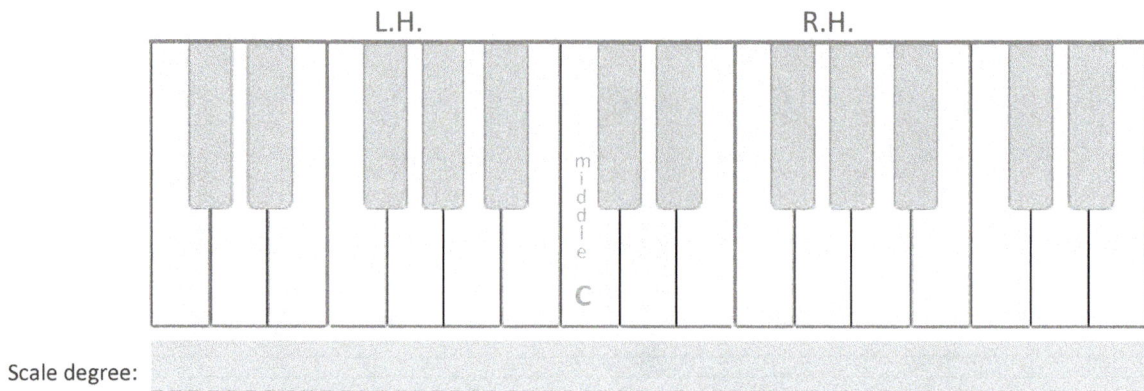

L.H.   R.H.

middle C

Scale degree:

5. Color the **G Major** position for both hands.

6. Write and circle the note-names of the 1st, 3rd, and 5th degrees on the keyboard for both hands. This is the **G Major** chord.

7. How many white keys between your two hand positions? _____

8. This chord uses _____ white key(s) and _____ black key(s).

▌▌▌ **Keyboard Activities**

9. Play a chord on the 1st and 2nd notes of the **G Major** pentascale. Which is your favorite?

10. How many half-steps between the notes G and B? _____ And between B and D?_____

Major Scale: 2 Major Tetrachords Connected with a Whole-Step

This is how we build it: W-W-H + W + W-W-H = major scale

tetrachord   tetrachord

Hint: Be sure to keep a half-step between the 3rd and 4th notes and the 7th and 8th notes.

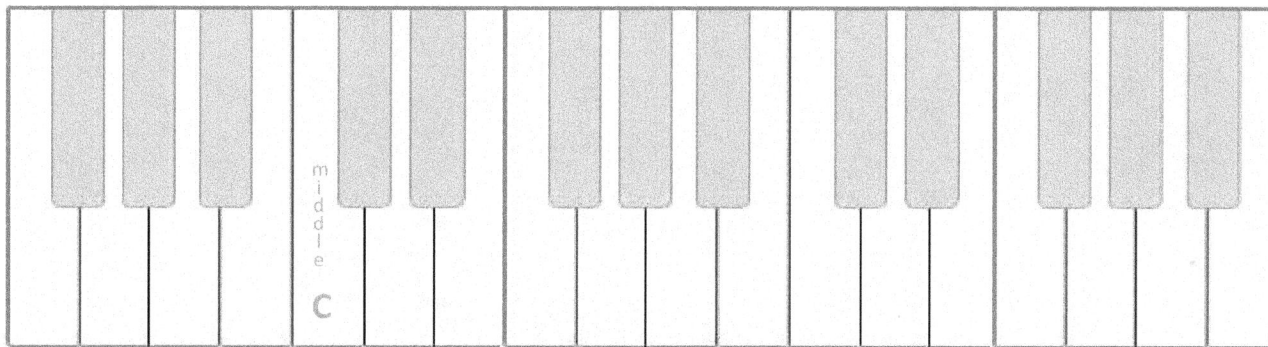

Scale degree:

W-H pattern:

chord notes

1. Start below middle C. Using the above formula, write each note from **G** to **G**.

2. Write the scale degrees. Identify the whole-steps (W) and the half-steps (H).

3. Color the half-steps in each tetrachord. They are: _____ to_____ and _____ to _____. What whole-step connects the two tetrachords? ____ to ____.

4. Above middle C, build a chord by using the 1st, 3rd, and 5th notes of the **G Major** scale. Write and circle the chord notes on the above keyboard. The notes of the **G Major** chord are: _____, _____, _____.

5. Write the chords in both clefs. Notice which chord uses line notes and which chord uses space notes.

L.H.   R.H.

G Major chords

G Major Key Signature

6. What black key is used in the **G Major** scale? _____

7. Play and say the **G Major** scale and chord. Memorize which black key it uses and notice how it is written in the key signature above.

| The chord built on the 1st note of the scale is called the **tonic** chord ($\underline{I}$) | The chord built on the 5th note of the scale is called the **dominant** chord ($\underline{V}$) |

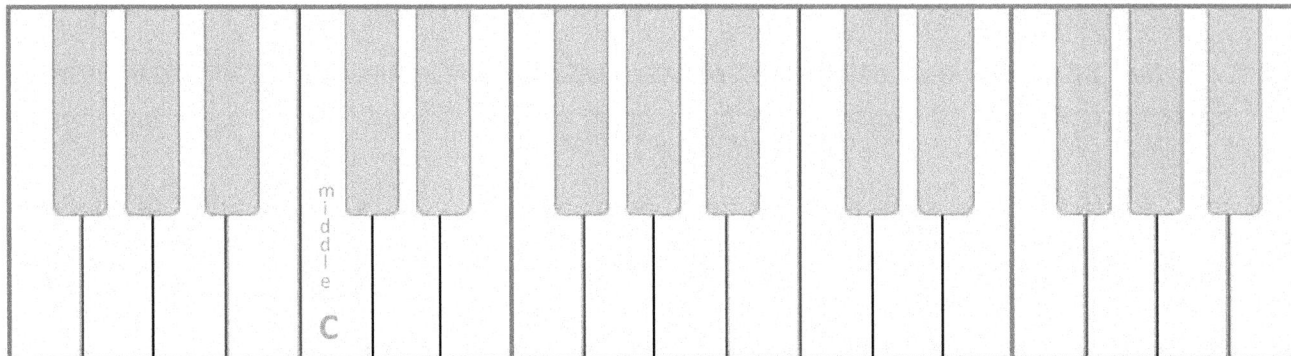

tonic chord + dominant chord + tonic chord = authentic cadence

| $\underline{I}$ | $\underline{V}$ | $\underline{I}$ | $\underline{I}$ | $\underline{V}$ | $\underline{I}$ |
| tonic | dominant | tonic | tonic | dominant | tonic |

Chord-name*:

* When you write major scales or chords, ALWAYS use capital letters.

▥ Keyboard Activities

1. Write the notes of the **G Major** position for the left hand. Circle the 1st and 5th notes.

2. Play a chord on the 1st note and a chord on the 5th note; then, write them on the staff above. These are the MOST important chords in the key of **G Major**.

3. Highlight the dominant chord on the keyboard starting on the 5th note of **G Major.**

4. The tonic note is _____ and its chord is on the _____degree of the scale.
   The dominant note is _____ and its chord is on the _____degree of the scale.

5. Hands alone, play back and forth between the tonic and dominant chords, then try playing them with both hands together.

6. Try playing a chord on every note of the **G Major** hand position. Remember to use F♯.
   How many chords used F♯?_____

Building the Parallel G Minor 5-Note Scale

g minor

Major: W-W-H - W

major tetrachord

Minor: W-H-W - W

minor tetrachord

The **major** 5-note scale has a half-step between the 3rd and 4th notes.

The **minor** 5-note scale has a half-step between the 2nd and 3rd notes.
(Move your 3rd finger down a half-step)

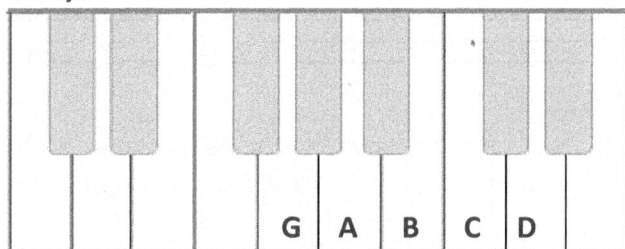

G Major

G A B C D

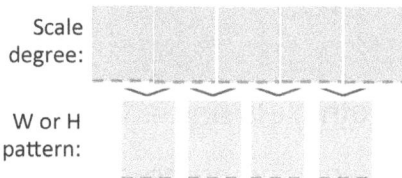

Scale degree:

W or H pattern:

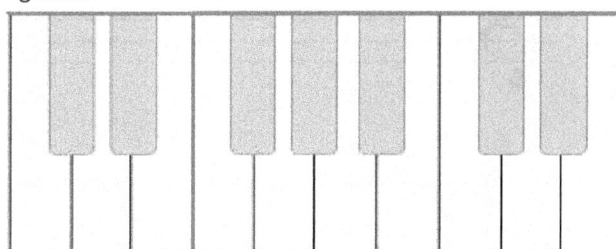

g minor

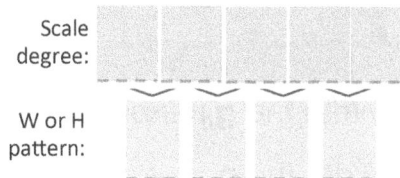

Scale degree:

W or H pattern:

1. On the left keyboard, write the scale degrees and W or H for the **G Major** 5-note scale.

2. Play the **G Major** pattern, but now lower the 3rd note by a half-step to create a half-step between the 2nd and 3rd notes.

3. What kind of accidental is used? _____ Name the lowered note: _____

4. Write the new **g minor** 5-note scale on the right keyboard. _____, _____, _____, _____, _____. (*ALWAYS use smaller lowercase letters for minor*).

5. What finger changes position? _____ Mark or color the half-steps on the keyboards above. The half-step in the 5-note **g minor** scale is between the notes ____ and ____. Notice where the half-step is between the major and minor tetrachords and how it changes the 5-note scales.

Keyboard Activities

6. This minor 5-note scale uses _____ white key(s) and _____ black key(s).

7. Which fingers play the black key in both hands? LH: _____ RH: _____

Building the G Minor Chord

(Left Hand)

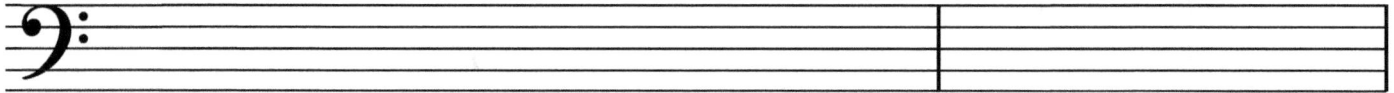

Note-name:

Finger-number:

g minor chord

(Right Hand)

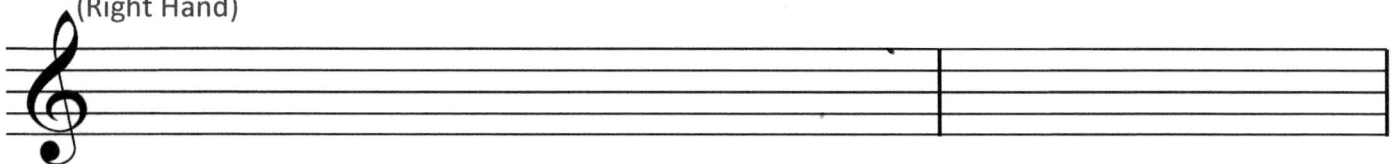

Note-name:

Finger-number:

g minor chord

1. Write the **g minor** pentascale (5-note scale) in both clefs and add any accidentals.

2. Write the note-names and the finger-numbers below the name of the notes.

3. Circle the two fingers and note-names with the half-step in each hand.

4. On the staff, highlight the 1st, 3rd, and 5th notes and write the chord on the staff. The notes of the **g minor** chord are: _____, _____, _____.

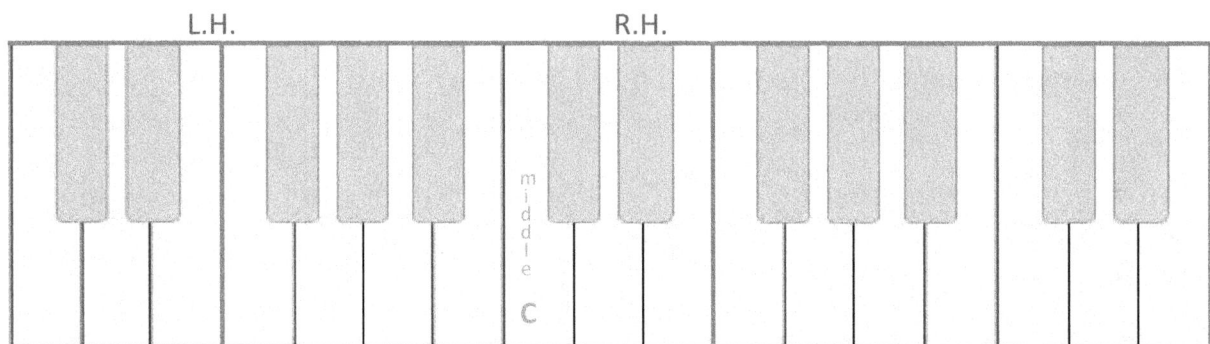

5. Write and highlight the notes of the **g minor** chord on the keyboard above.

6. While at the keyboard, practice switching from **g minor** to **G Major**. Notice how your hand position changes as you move the 3rd finger from the b♭ to the B♮.

How we build it: **W-H-W + W-H-W + W** = natural minor scale

▌▌▌ Keyboard Activities

Looking at the **G Major** scale and key signature (see page 11), do the following:

1. What is the 6th note of the **G Major** scale? _____. Highlight the note on the left keyboard below.

2. Using the same notes and accidentals, play a scale on the 6th note of the **G Major** scale to make *the relative natural minor scale of G Major*. Notice it uses the same notes and keys as **G Major**, but begins and ends on the note E (the 6th note of **G Major**).

3. The **G Major** and **e minor** scales use _____ white key(s) and _____ black key(s). They are *relative scales* because they contain the same notes and use the same key signature.

G Major scale

G A B C D E F♯ G

Scale degree:

W-H pattern:

____ minor scale (highlight the 5-note scale)

Scale degree:

W-H pattern:

4. Using the same notes as **G Major**, but starting on the note E, write the scale on the keyboard diagram. Highlight the new 5-note **e minor** scale.
    The notes are: _____, _____, _____, _____, _____.

5. How many sharps does **e minor** have? _____ Circle and name the sharp: _____

6. Circle the scale degrees and keyboard notes where the half-steps are in both of these relative scales. Notice how they are different. The half-steps in the **e natural minor** scale are between the scale degrees: _____ & _____, and _____ & _____; and between the notes: _____ & _____, and _____ & _____.

Building the E Minor Chord

1. Write the **e minor** pentascale (5-note scale) in both clefs and add any accidentals.

2. Write the finger-numbers and note-names below the staff. Circle the 1st, 3rd, and 5th fingerings and note-names in each hand.

3. Circle and highlight the 1st, 3rd, and 5th notes and write the chord on the staff. The notes of the **e minor** chord are: _____, _____, _____.

(Left Hand)   (Right Hand)

Finger-number: e min chord   e min chord

Note-names:

4. Highlight and write the notes of the **e minor** chord on the keyboard below.

5. How many half-steps are between the note E and the note G? _____

6. How many half-steps are between the note G and the note B? _____

7. What notes are shared in the **G Major** and **e minor** chord? _____ & _____

L.H.   R.H.

middle C

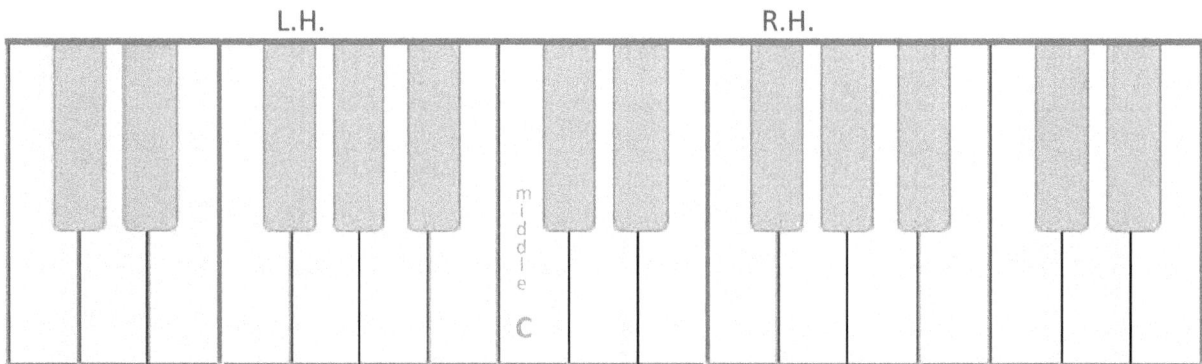

Challenge Activities

Remember the accidental!

Building chords on the **G Major** scale, remember to use F♯. (Circle the correct answer)

8. Play a chord on the 2nd note of **G Major**. Is it major or minor?

9. Play a chord on the 3rd note of **G Major**. Is it major or minor?

10. Play a chord on the 4th note of **G Major**. Is it major or minor?

11. Play a chord on the 5th note of **G Major**. Is it major or minor?

Major Tetrachord + Whole-Step
(W - W - H)   +   (W)

1. Write the **D Major** pentascale (5-note scale) in both clefs and add any accidentals. (Write the major note names in capital letters.)

2. Mark the half-steps and the whole-steps on the second line.

3. Write the finger-numbers. Circle the fingerings and note-names with half-steps in each hand, and on the staff.

4. Highlight the 1st, 3rd, and 5th notes on each staff.

(Left Hand)

Note-name:

W-H pattern:

Finger-number:

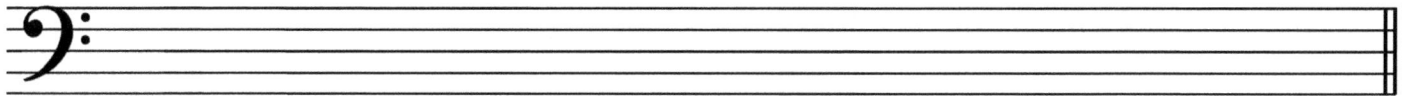

(Right Hand)

Note-name:

W-H pattern:

Finger-number:

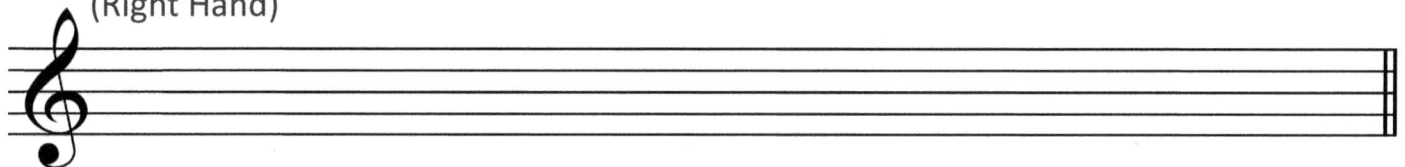

| Keyboard Activities

5. Play your **D Major** *5-note* scale up and down, using staccato notes.

6. Play your 5-note scale with half notes and then with quarter notes.

7. This 5-note scale uses _____ white keys and the black key _____.

Learning D Major Hand Position

L.H.   R.H.

Fingering: 5 4   2 1   1 2   4 5

Note-Name:

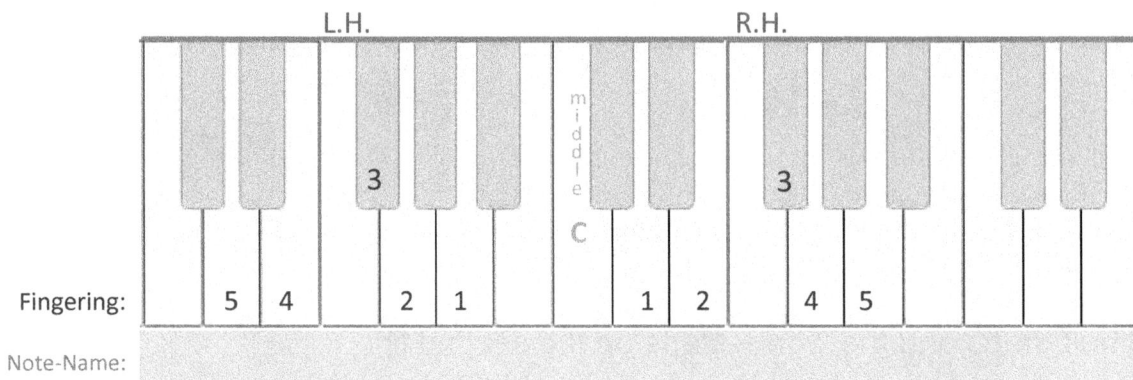

1. Write each note of the **D Major** position below the keyboard diagram.

2. Highlight the **D Major** pentascale above and below middle C.

3. Circle the note-names and fingerings of the half-step in each hand.

4. The half-step is between the notes _____ and _____. This hand position stretches from the notes _____ to _____.

L.H.   R.H.

Scale degree:

5. Color the **D Major** position for both hands.

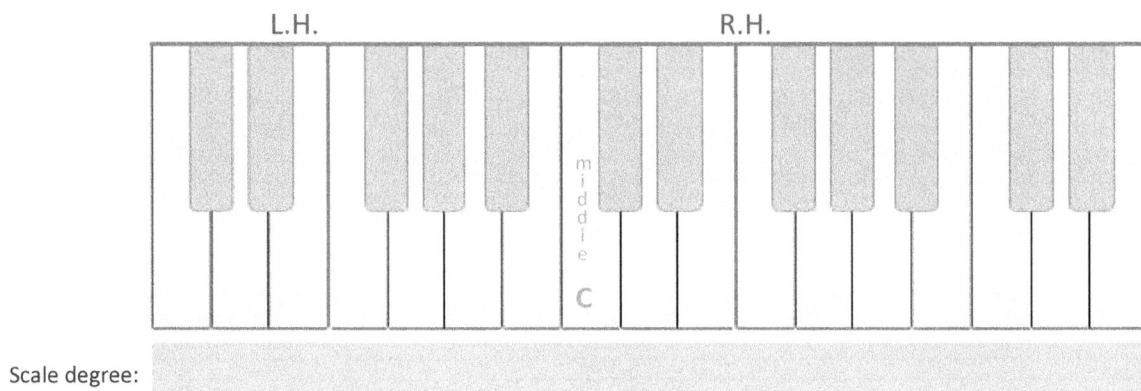

6. Write and circle the note names of the 1st, 3rd, and 5th degrees on the keyboard for both hands. This is the **D Major** chord.

7. How many white keys between your two hand positions? _____

8. This chord uses _____ white key(s) and _____ black key(s): _____

Keyboard Activities

9. Play a chord on the 1st and 2nd note of the **D Major** pentascale. Which is your favorite?

10. How many half-steps between the notes D and F♯? _____ And between F♯ and A?_____

Building the 8-Note D Major Scale

D Major Scale

Major Scale= 2 Major Tetrachords <u>Connected</u> with a Whole-Step

This is how we build it: W-W-H + **W** + W-W-H = major scale

tetrachord   tetrachord

Hint: Be sure to keep a half-step between the 3rd and 4th notes and the 7th and 8th notes.

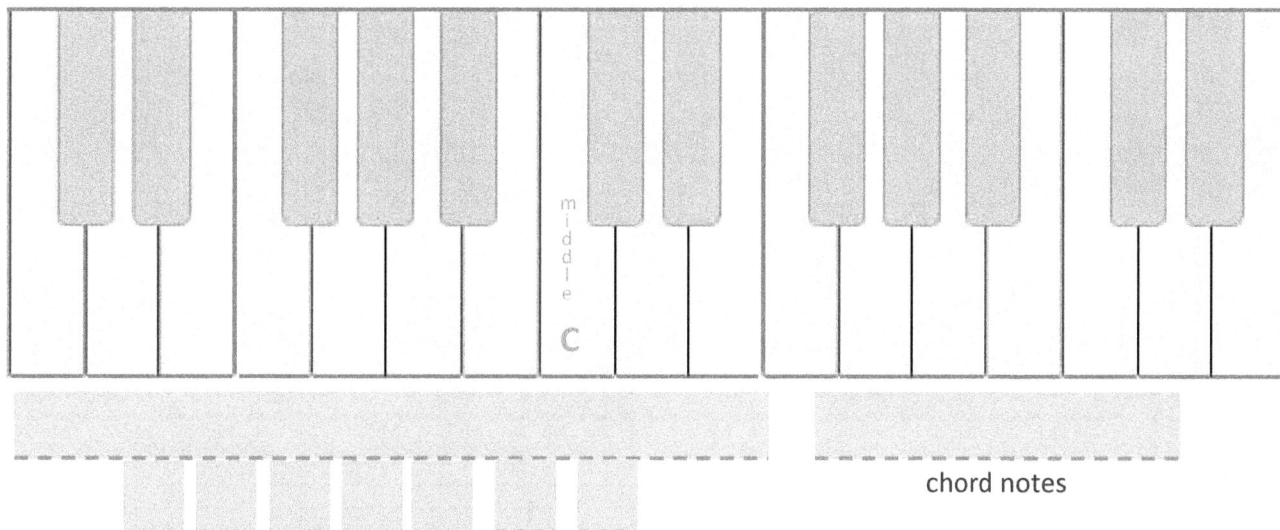

Scale degree:

W-H pattern:

middle C

chord notes

1. Start below middle C. Using the above formula, write each note from **D** to **D**.

2. Write the scale degrees. Identify the whole-steps (W) and the half-steps (H).

3. Color the half-steps in each tetrachord. They are: _____ to_____ and _____ to _____. What whole-step connects the two tetrachords? _____ to _____.

4. Above middle C, build a chord by writing the 1st, 3rd, and 5th notes of the **D Major** scale. Write and circle the chord notes on the above keyboard. The notes of the **D Major** chord are: _____, _____, _____.

5. Write the chords in both clefs. Notice which chord uses line notes and which chord uses space notes.

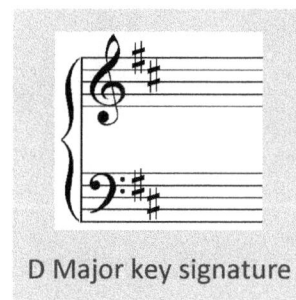

L.H.   R.H.

D Major chords

D Major key signature

6. What black keys are used in the **D Major** scale? _____ and _____.

7. Play and say the **D Major** scale and chord. Memorize which sharps are used and notice how they are written in the above key signature.

Writing Essentials for the Beginner Pianist Copyright © 2014 Clara Castano & Catherine A. Thompson

19

How to Build an Authentic Cadence ($\bar{V}$-$\bar{I}$) in D Major

The chord built on the 1st note of the scale is called the **tonic** chord ($\bar{I}$)	The chord built on the 5th note of the scale is called the **dominant** chord ($\bar{V}$)

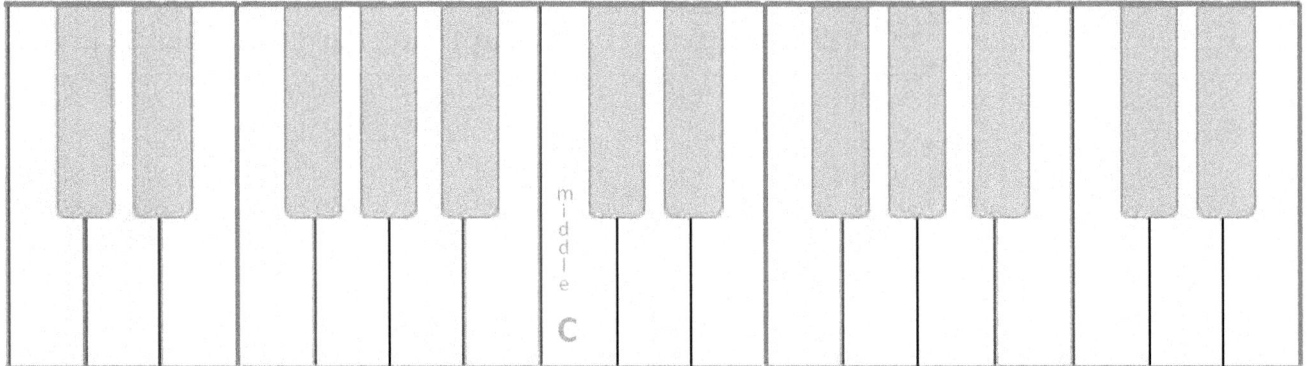

tonic chord + dominant chord + tonic chord = authentic cadence

Chord-name*:

$\bar{I}$	$\bar{V}$	$\bar{I}$	$\bar{I}$	$\bar{V}$	$\bar{I}$
tonic	dominant	tonic	tonic	dominant	tonic

* When you write major scales or chords, ALWAYS use capital letters.

🎹 Keyboard Activities

1. Write the notes of the **D Major** position for the left hand. Circle the 1st and 5th notes.

2. Play a chord on the 1st note and a chord on the 5th note. Then, write them on the keys and staff above. These are the MOST important chords in the key of **D Major**.

3. Highlight the dominant chord on the keyboard starting on the 5th note of **D Major.**

4. The tonic note is _____ and its chord is on the _____degree of the scale.
   The dominant note is _____ and its chord is on the _____degree of the scale.

5. Hands alone, play back and forth between the tonic and dominant chords, then try playing them with both hands together.

6. If you play a chord on every note of the **D Major** scale, how many chords are using any of the black keys F♯ and C♯?_____

Major: W-W-H - W	Minor: W-H-W - W
major tetrachord	minor tetrachord

The **major** 5-note scale has a half-step between the 3rd and 4th notes.

The **minor** 5-note scale has a half-step between the 2nd and 3rd notes.
(Move your 3rd finger down a half-step)

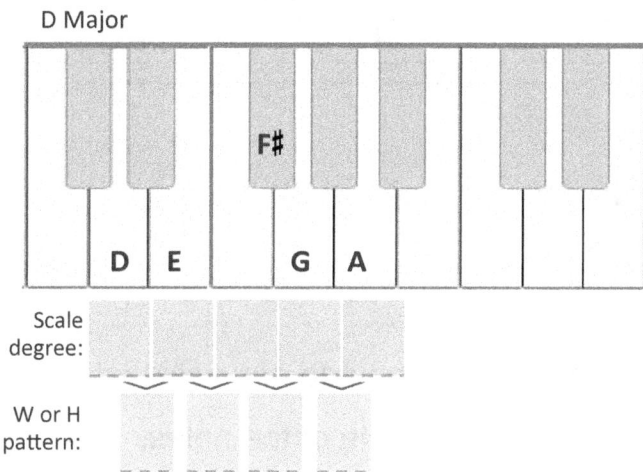

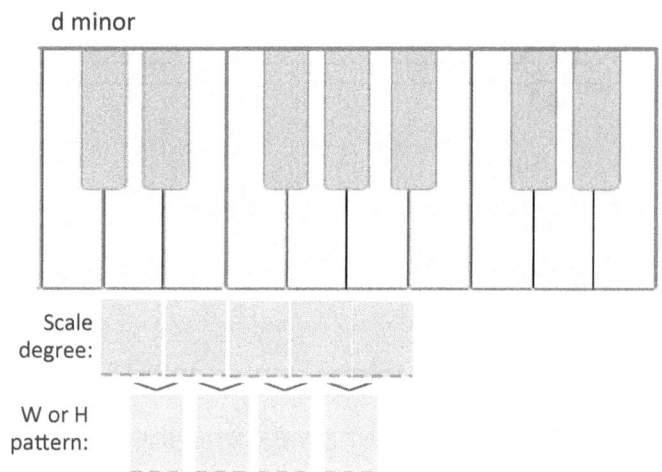

D Major

F#

D E   G A

Scale degree:

W or H pattern:

d minor

Scale degree:

W or H pattern:

1. On the left keyboard, write the scale degrees and W or H for the **D Major** 5-note scale.

2. Play the **D Major** pattern, but now lower the 3rd note by a half-step to create a half-step between the 2nd and 3rd notes.

3. What kind of accidental is used? _____ Name the lowered note: _____

4. Write the new **d minor** 5-note scale on the right keyboard. _____, _____, _____, _____, _____ (*ALWAYS use smaller lowercase letters for minor*).

5. What finger changes position? _____ Mark or color the half-steps on the keyboards above. The half-step in the 5-note **d minor** scale is between the notes ____ and _____. Notice where the half-step is between the major and minor tetrachords and how it changes the 5-note scales.

▌▌▌ Keyboard Activities

6. This minor 5-note scale uses _____ white key(s) and _____ black key(s).

7. Which fingers play the F-natural in both hands? LH:_____   RH: _____

Building the D Minor Chord

(Left Hand)

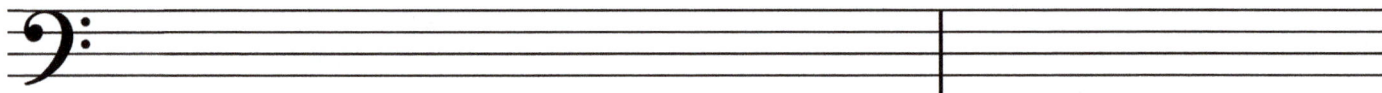

Note-name:

Finger-number:

d minor chord

(Right Hand)

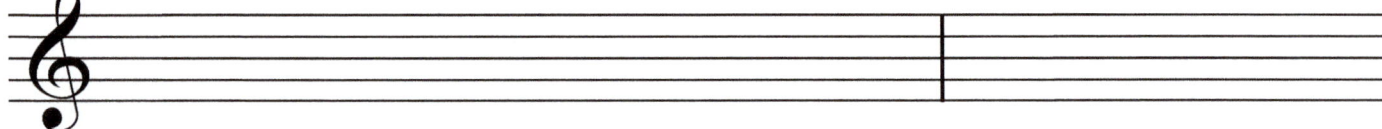

Note-name:

Finger-number:

d minor chord

1. Write the **d minor** pentascale (5-note scale) in both clefs and add any accidentals.

2. Write the note-names and the finger-numbers below the name of the notes.

3. Circle the two fingers and note-names with the half-step in each hand.

4. On the staff, highlight the 1st, 3rd, and 5th notes and write the chord on the staff. The notes of the **d minor** chord are: _____, _____, _____.

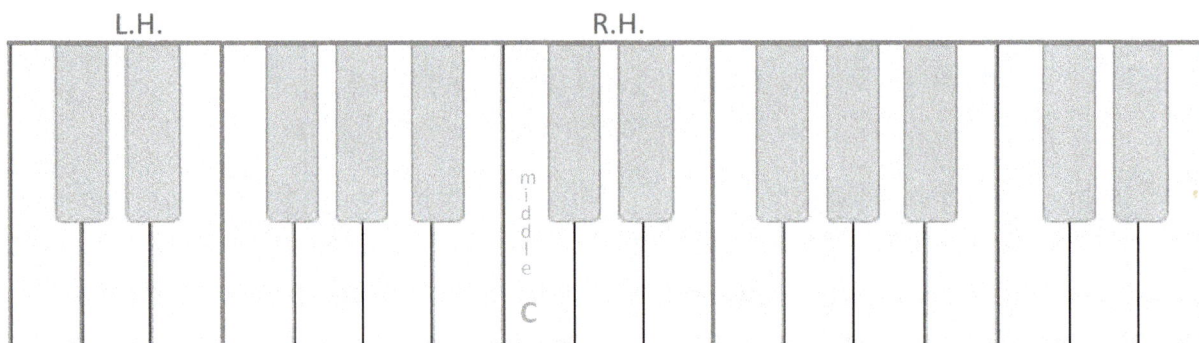

L.H.   R.H.

middle C

5. Write and highlight the notes of the **d minor** chord on the keyboard above.

6. While at your own keyboard, practice switching from **d minor** to **D Major**. Notice how your hand position changes as you move the 3rd finger from the ♮ to the **F♯**.

D Major's Relative Minor Scale is *B Natural Minor*

> How we build it: **W-H-W + W-H-W + W** = natural minor scale

⊞ Keyboard Activities

Looking at the **D Major** scale and key signature (see page 19), do the following:

1. What is the 6th note of the **D Major** scale? _____. Highlight the note on the left keyboard below.

2. Using the same notes and accidentals, play a scale on the 6th note of the **D Major** scale to make *the relative natural minor scale of D Major*. Notice it uses the same notes and keys as **D Major**, but begins and ends on the note B (the 6th note of **D Major**).

3. The **D Major** and **b minor** scales use _____ white key(s) and _____ black key(s). They are *relative scales* because they contain the same notes and use the same key signature.

D Major scale

| | | | F# | | | C# | |
| D | E | | G | A | B | | D |

Scale degree:

W-H pattern:

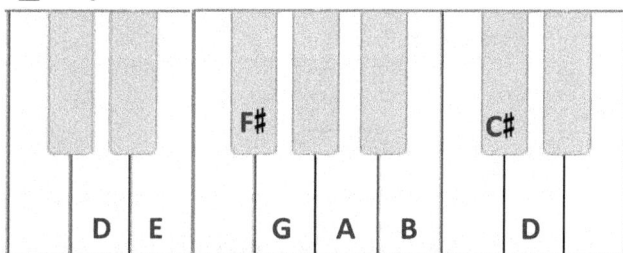

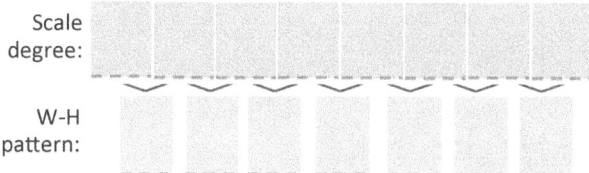

_____ minor scale (highlight the 5-note scale)

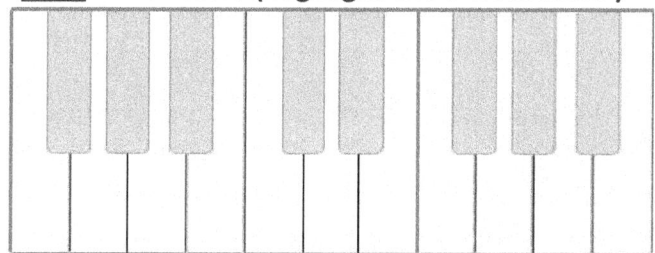

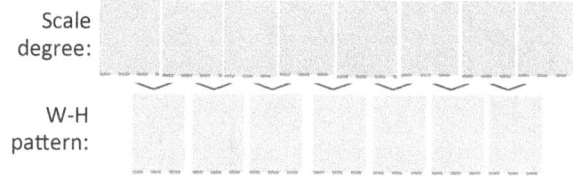

Scale degree:

W-H pattern:

4. Using the same notes as **D Major**, but starting on the note B, write the scale on the keyboard diagram. Highlight the new 5-note **b minor** scale.
   The notes are: _____, _____, _____, _____, _____.

5. How many sharps does **b minor** have? ____Circle and name the sharps: _____,_____.

6. Circle the scale degrees and keyboard notes where the half-steps are in both of these relative scales. Notice how they are different. The half-steps in the **b natural minor** scale are between the scale degrees: _____ & _____, and _____ & _____; and between the notes: _____ & _____, and _____ & _____.

Building the B Minor Chord

1. Write the **b minor** pentascale (5-note scale) in both clefs and add any accidentals.

2. Write the finger-numbers and note-names below the staff. Circle the 1st, 3rd, and 5th fingerings and note-names in each hand.

3. Circle and highlight the 1st, 3rd, and 5th notes and write the chord on the staff. The notes of the **b minor** chord are: _____, _____, _____.

(Left Hand)   (Right Hand)

Finger-number: _____   b min chord   b min chord

Note-names: _____

4. Highlight and write the notes of the **b minor** chord on the keyboard below.

5. How many half-steps are between the note B and the note D? _____

6. How many half-steps are between the note D and the note F♯? _____

7. What notes are shared in the **D Major** and **b minor** chord? _____ & _____

middle C

Remember the accidentals!

Challenge Activities

Building chords on the **D Major** scale, remember to use F♯, C♯ (Circle the correct answer)

8. Play a chord on the 2nd note of **D Major**. Is it major or minor?

9. Play a chord on the 3rd note of **D Major**. Is it major or minor?

10. Play a chord on the 4th note of **D Major**. Is it major or minor?

11. Play a chord on the 5th note of **D Major**. Is it major or minor?

Major Tetrachord + Whole-Step
(W - W - H)   +   (W)

1. Write the **A Major** pentascale (5-note scale) in both clefs and add any accidentals. (Write the major note names in capital letters.)

2. Mark the half-steps and the whole-steps on the second line.

3. Write the finger-numbers. Circle the fingerings and note-names with half-steps in each hand, and on the staff.

4. Highlight the 1st, 3rd, and 5th notes on each staff.

(Left Hand)

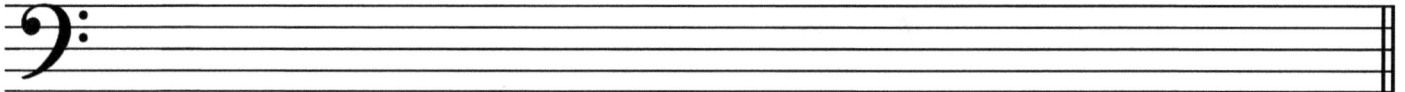

Note-name:

W-H pattern:

Finger-number:

(Right Hand)

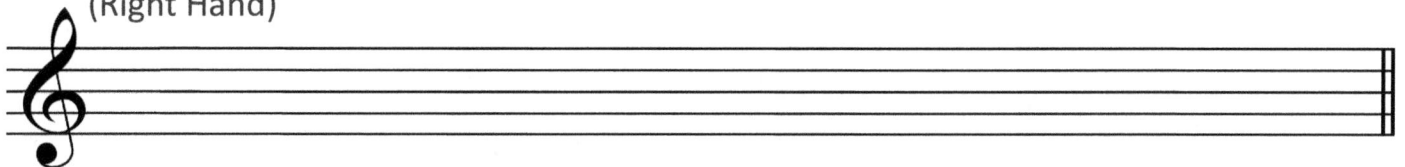

Note-name:

W-H pattern:

Finger-number:

Keyboard Activities

5. Play your **A Major** 5-note scale up and down, using staccato notes.

6. Play your 5-note scale with half notes and then with quarter notes.

7. This 5-note scale uses _____ white keys and the black key _____ .

Learning A Major Hand Position

L.H.   R.H.

middle C

| | | | 3 | | | | | 3 |

Fingering: 5 4   2 1   1 2   4 5

Note-Name:

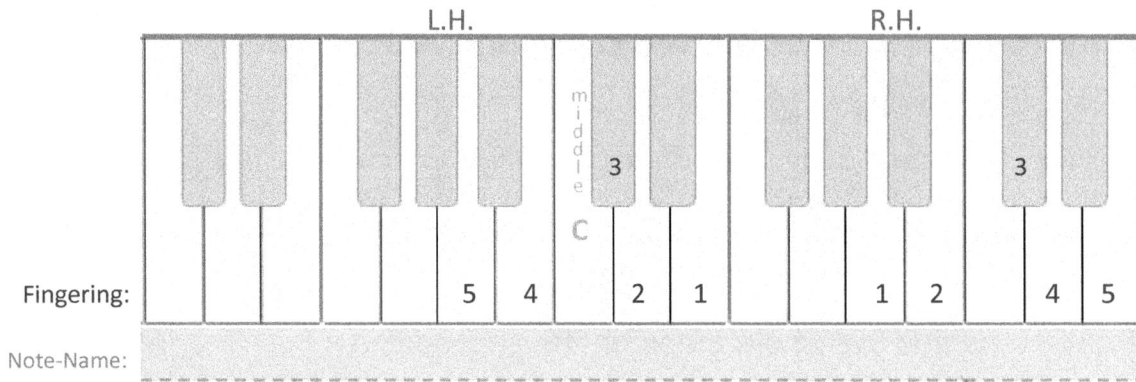

1. Write each note of the **A Major** position below the keyboard diagram.

2. Highlight the **A Major** pentascale above and below middle C.

3. Circle the note-names and fingerings of the half-step in each hand.

4. The half-step is between the notes _____ and _____. This hand position stretches from the notes _____ to _____.

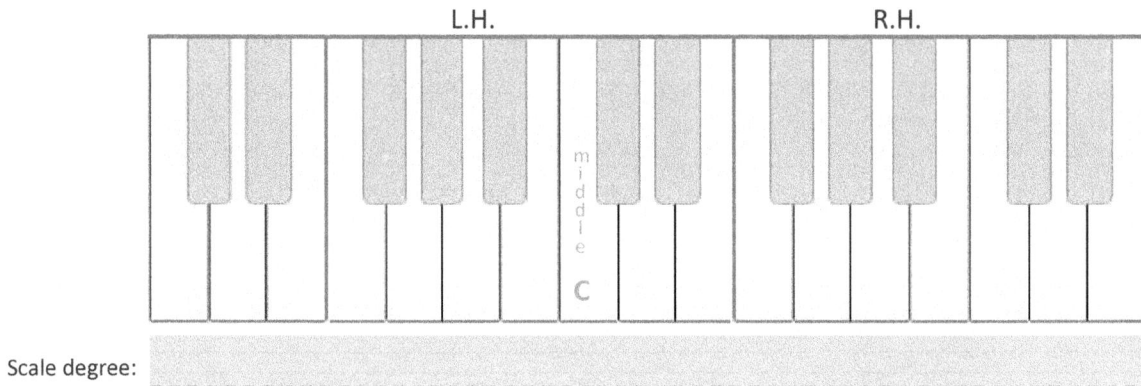

L.H.   R.H.

middle C

Scale degree:

5. Color the **A Major** position for both hands.

6. Write and circle the note-names of the 1st, 3rd, and 5th degrees on the keyboard for both hands. This is the **A Major** chord.

7. How many white keys between your two hand positions? _____

8. This chord uses _____ white key(s) and _____ black key(s): _____

|||| Keyboard Activities

9. Play a chord on the 1st and 2nd note of the **A Major** pentascale. Which is your favorite?

10. How many half-steps between the notes A and C♯? _____ And between C♯ and E? _____

Major Scale: 2 Major Tetrachords Connected with a Whole-Step

This is how we build it: W-W-H + W + W-W-H = major scale

tetrachord   tetrachord

Hint: Be sure to keep a half-step between the 3rd and 4th notes and the 7th and 8th notes.

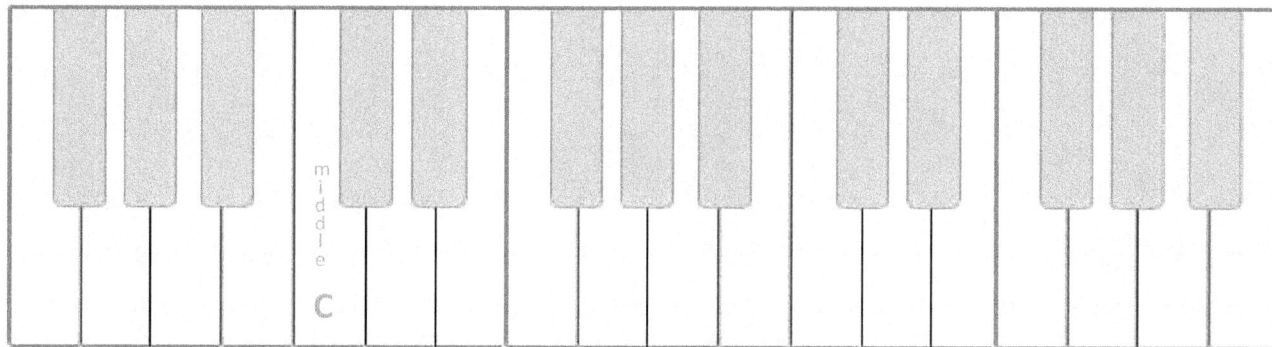

Scale degree:

W-H pattern:

chord notes

1. Start below middle C. Using the above formula, write each note from **A** to **A**.

2. Write the scale degrees. Identify the whole-steps (W) and the half-steps (H).

3. Color the half-steps in each tetrachord. They are: _____ to_____ and _____ to _____.
   What whole-step connects the two tetrachords? ____ to ____.

4. Above middle C, build a chord by writing the 1st, 3rd, and 5th notes of the **A Major** scale.
   Write and circle the chord notes on the above keyboard.
   The notes of the **A Major** chord are: _____, _____, _____.

5. Write the chords in both clefs. Notice which chord uses line notes
   and which chord uses space notes.

L.H.   R.H.

A Major chords

A Major key signature

6. What black keys are used in the **A Major** scale? _____, _____ and _____.

7. Play and say the **A Major** scale and chord. Memorize which sharps are used
   and notice how they are written in the above key signature.

How to Build an Authentic Cadence ($\overline{\underline{V}}$-$\underline{I}$) in A Major

Cadences

The chord built on the 1st note of the scale is called the **tonic** chord ($\underline{I}$)

The chord built on the 5th note of the scale is called the **dominant** chord ($\overline{\underline{V}}$)

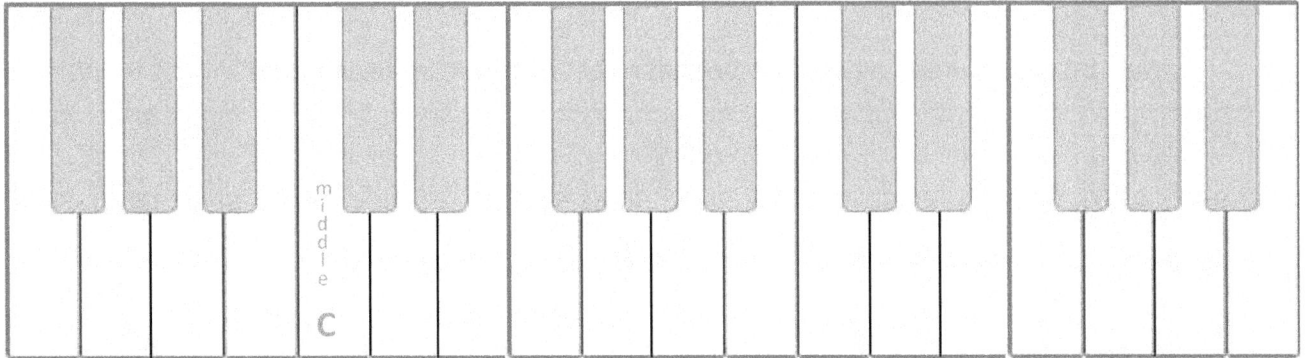

tonic chord **+** dominant chord **+** tonic chord **=** authentic cadence

Chord-name*:

tonic   dominant   tonic   tonic   dominant   tonic

* When you write major scales or chords, ALWAYS use capital letters.

Keyboard Activities

1. Write the notes of the **A Major** position for the left hand. Circle the 1st and 5th notes.

2. Play a chord on the 1st note and a chord on the 5th note. Then, write them on the keys and staff above. These are the MOST important chords in the key of **A Major**.

3. Highlight the dominant chord on the keyboard starting on the 5th note of **A Major.**

4. The tonic note is _____ and its chord is on the _____ degree of the scale.
   The dominant note is _____ and its chord is on the _____ degree of the scale.

5. Hands alone, play back and forth between the tonic and dominant chords, then try playing them with both hands together.

6. If you play a chord on every note of the **A Major** scale, how many chords are using any of the black keys F♯, C♯, and G♯?_____

Writing Essentials for the Beginner Pianist Copyright © 2014 Clara Castano & Catherine A. Thompson   28

Building the Parallel A Minor 5-Note Scale

Major: W-W-H - W

major tetrachord

Minor: W-H-W - W

minor tetrachord

> The **major** 5-note scale has a half-step between the 3rd and 4th notes.

> The **minor** 5-note scale has a half-step between the 2nd and 3rd notes.
> (Move your 3rd finger down a half-step)

A Major

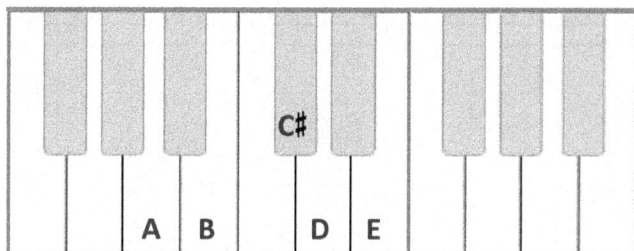

Scale degree:

W or H pattern:

a minor

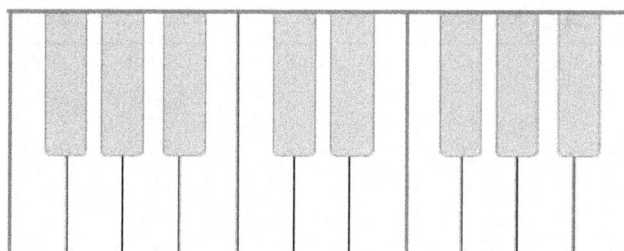

Scale degree:

W or H pattern:

1. On the left keyboard, write the scale degrees and W or H for the **A Major** 5-note scale.

2. Play the **A Major** pattern, but now lower the 3rd note by a half-step to create a half-step between the 2nd and 3rd notes.

3. What kind of accidental is used? _____ Name the lowered note: _____

4. Write the new **a minor** 5-note scale on the right keyboard. _____, _____, _____, _____, _____ (*ALWAYS use smaller lowercase letters for minor*).

5. What finger changes position? _____ Mark or color the half-steps on the keyboards above. The half-step in the 5-note **a minor** scale is between the notes ____ and ____. Notice where the half-step is between the major and minor tetrachords and how it changes the 5-note scales.

▌▌▌ Keyboard Activities

6. This minor 5-note scale uses _____ white key(s) and _____ black key(s).

7. Which fingers play the C-natural in both hands? LH:_____ RH: _____

Building the A Minor Chord

(Left Hand)

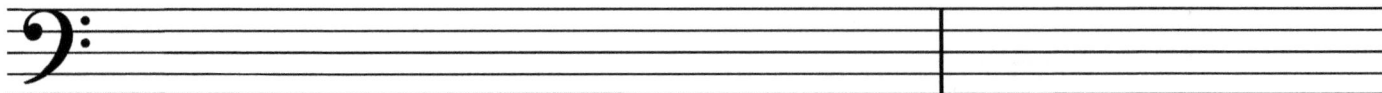

Note-name:

Finger-number:

a minor chord

(Right Hand)

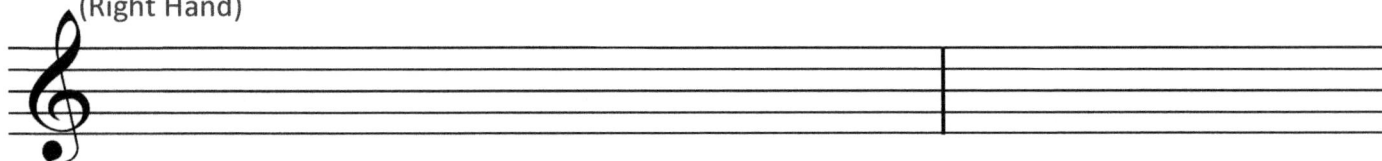

Note-name:

Finger-number:

a minor chord

1. Write the **a minor** pentascale (5-note scale) in both clefs and add any accidentals.

2. Write the note-names and the finger-numbers below the name of the notes.

3. Circle the two fingers and note-names with the half-step in each hand.

4. On the staff, highlight the 1st, 3rd, and 5th notes and write the chord on the staff. The notes of the **a minor** chord are: _____, _____, _____. Do you remember what other major key is related to the **a minor** chord? _____ Major.

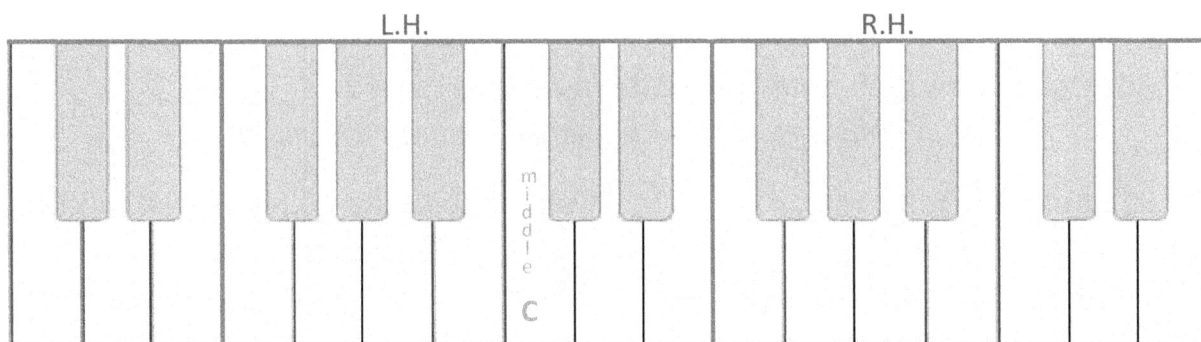

5. Write and highlight the notes of the **a minor** chord on the keyboard above.

6. While at your own keyboard, practice switching from **a minor** to **A Major**. Notice how your hand position changes as you move the 3rd finger from the c♮ to the **C♯**.

A Major's Relative Minor Scale is *F♯ Natural Minor*

f♯ minor scale

How we build it: **W-H-W + W-H-W + W** = natural minor scale

▌▌▌ Keyboard Activities

Looking at the **A Major** scale and key signature (see page 27), do the following:

1. What is the 6th note of the **A Major** scale? _____. Highlight the note on the left keyboard below.

2. Using the same notes and accidentals, play a scale on the 6th note of the **A Major** scale to make *the relative natural minor scale of A Major*. Notice it uses the same notes and keys as **A Major**, but begins and ends on the note F♯ (the 6th note of **A Major**).

3. The **A Major** and **f♯ minor** scales use _____ white key(s) and _____ black key(s). They are *relative scales* because they contain the same notes and use the same key signature.

A Major scale

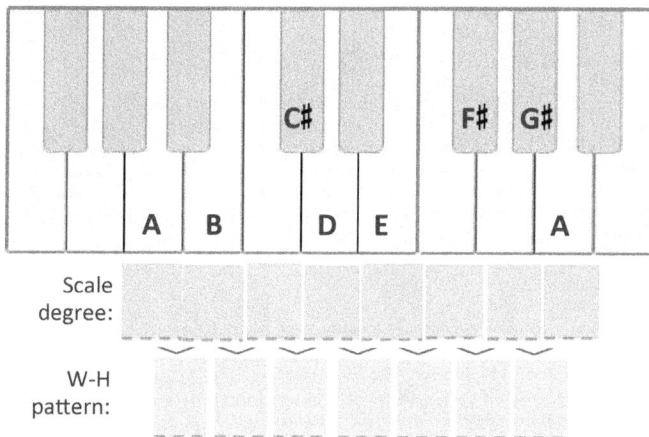

_____ minor scale (highlight the 5-note scale)

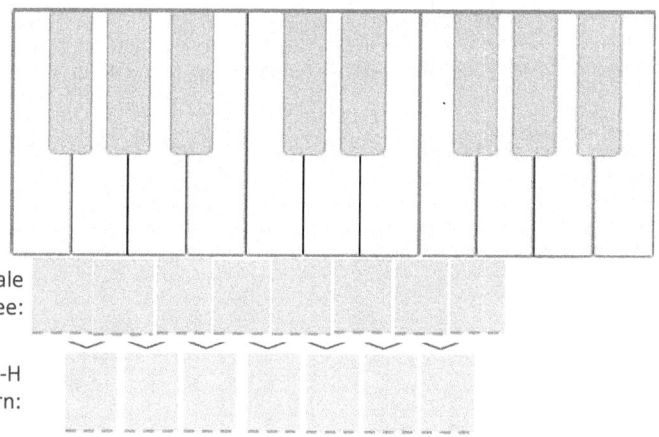

4. Using the same notes as **A Major**, but starting on the note F♯, write the scale on the keyboard diagram. Highlight the new 5-note **f♯ minor** scale.
   The notes are: _____, _____, _____, _____, _____.

5. How many sharps does **f♯ minor** have? _____
   Circle and name the sharps: _____, _____, _____.

6. Circle the scale degrees and keyboard notes where the half-steps are in both of these relative scales. Notice how they are different. The half-steps in the **f♯ natural minor** scale are between the scale degrees: _____ & _____, and _____ & _____; and between the notes: _____ & _____, and _____ & _____.

Writing Essentials for the Beginner Pianist Copyright © 2014 Clara Castano & Catherine A. Thompson   **31**

Building the F♯ Minor Chord

1. Write the **f♯ minor** pentascale (5-note scale) in both clefs and add any accidentals.

2. Write the finger-numbers and note-names below the staff. Circle the 1st, 3rd, and 5th fingerings and note-names in each hand.

3. Circle and highlight the 1st, 3rd, and 5th notes and write the chord on the staff.
   The notes of the **f♯ minor** chord are: _____, _____, _____.

(Left Hand)   (Right Hand)

Finger-number: f♯ min chord   f♯ min chord

Note-names:

4. Highlight and write the notes of the **f♯ minor** chord on the keyboard below.

5. How many half-steps are between the note F♯ and the note A? _____

6. How many half-steps are between the note A and the note C♯? _____

7. What notes are shared in the **A Major** and **f♯ minor** chord? _____ & _____

middle C

Remember the accidentals!

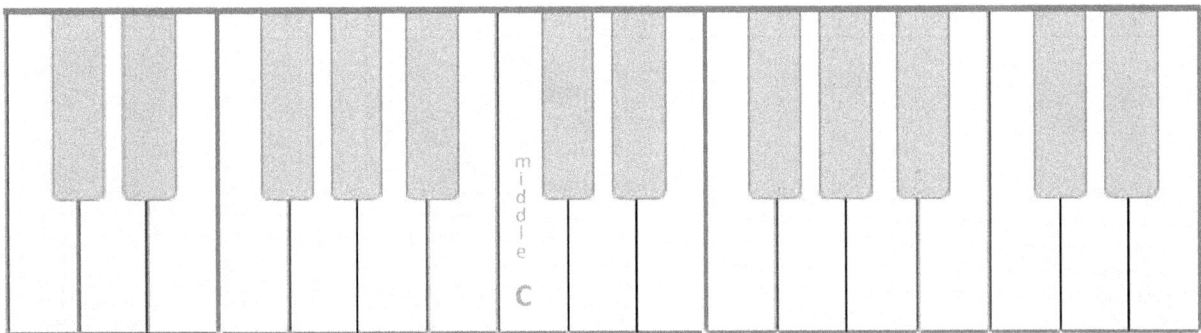

Challenge Activities

Building chords on the **A Major** scale, remember F♯, C♯, G♯. (Circle the correct answer)

8. Play a chord on the 2nd note of **A Major**. Is it major or minor?

9. Play a chord on the 3rd note of **A Major**. Is it major or minor?

10. Play a chord on the 4th note of **A Major**. Is it major or minor?

11. Play a chord on the 5th note of **A Major**. Is it major or minor?

Major Tetrachord + Whole-Step
(W - W - H)   +   (W)

1. Write the **E Major** pentascale (5-note scale) in both clefs and add any accidentals. (Write the major note names in capital letters.)

2. Mark the half-steps and the whole-steps on the second line.

3. Write the finger-numbers. Circle the fingerings and note-names with half-steps in each hand, and on the staff.

4. Highlight the 1st, 3rd, and 5th notes on each staff.

(Left Hand)

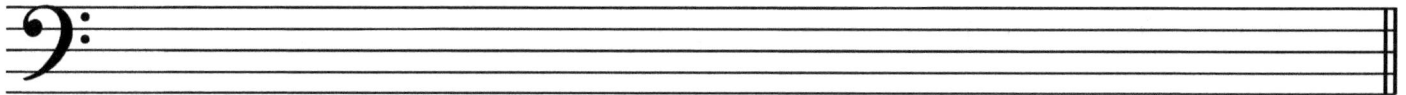

Note-name:

W-H pattern:

Finger-number:

(Right Hand)

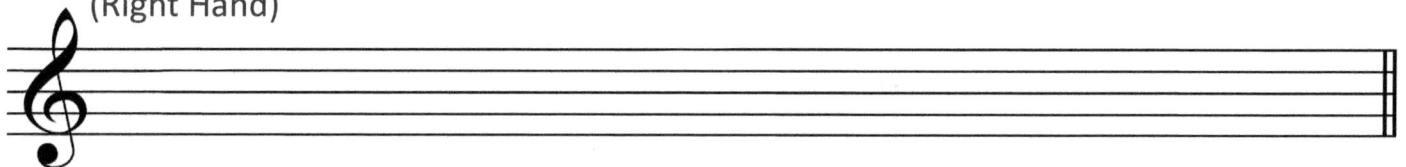

Note-name:

W-H pattern:

Finger-number:

▌▌▌ Keyboard Activities

5. Play your **E Major** 5-note scale up and down, using staccato notes.

6. Play your 5-note scale with half notes and then with quarter notes.

7. This 5-note scale uses _____ white keys and the black keys _____ and _____.

Learning E Major Hand Position

L.H.   R.H.

Fingering:

Note-Name:

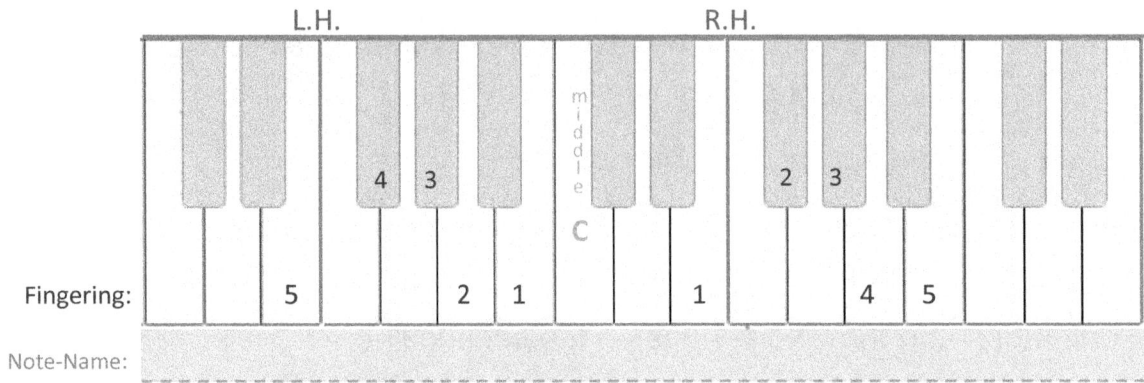

1. Write each note of the **E Major** position below the keyboard diagram.

2. Highlight the **E Major** pentascale above and below middle C.

3. Circle the note-names and fingerings of the half-step in each hand.

4. The half-step is between the notes _____ and _____. This hand position stretches from the notes _____ to _____.

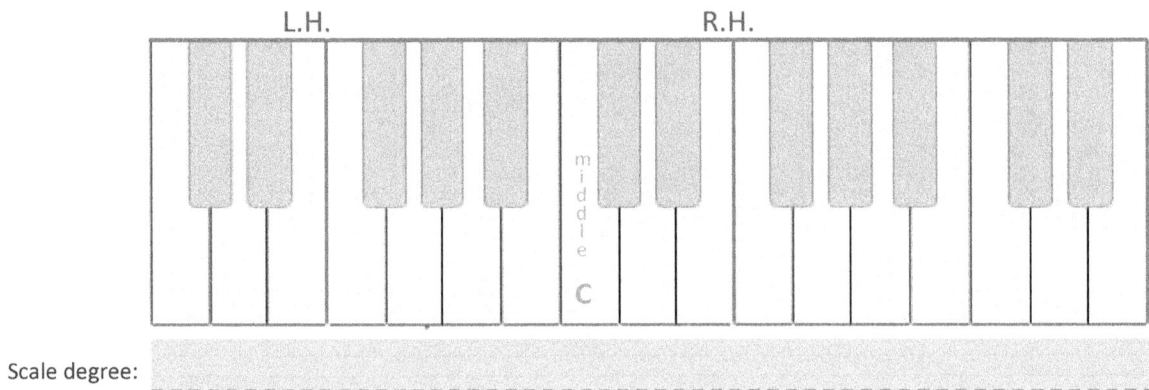

L.H.   R.H.

Scale degree:

5. Color the **E Major** position for both hands.

6. Write and circle the note-names of the 1st, 3rd, and 5th degrees on the keyboard for both hands. This is the **E Major** chord.

7. How many white keys between your two hand positions? _____

8. This chord uses _____ white key(s) and _____ black key(s): _____.

▐▌▌ Keyboard Activities

9. Play a chord on the 1st and 2nd note of the **E Major** pentascale. Which is your favorite?

10. How many half-steps between the notes E and G♯? _____ And between G♯ and B?_____

Major Scale= 2 Major Tetrachords <u>Connected</u> with a Whole-Step

This is how we build it:	W-W-H	+	**W**	+	W-W-H	= major scale

tetrachord   tetrachord

Hint: Be sure to keep a half-step between the 3rd and 4th notes and the 7th and 8th notes.

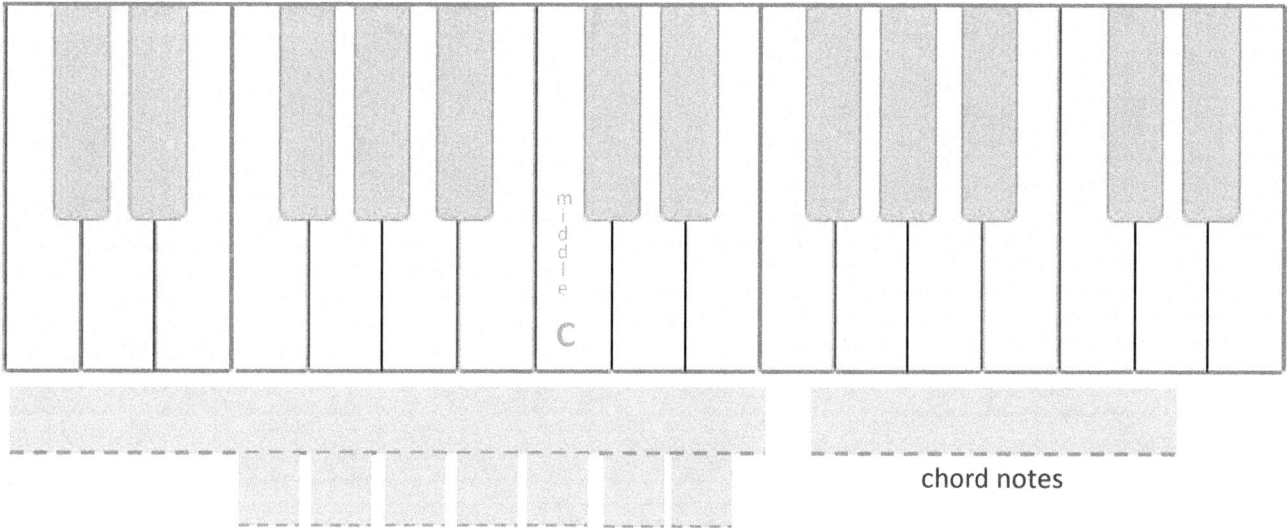

Scale degree:

W-H pattern:

middle C

chord notes

1. Start below middle C. Using the above formula, write each note from **E** to **E**.

2. Write the scale degrees. Identify the whole-steps (W) and the half-steps (H).

3. Color the half-steps in each tetrachord. They are: _____ to_____ and _____ to _____.
    What whole-step connects the two tetrachords? _____ to _____.

4. Above middle C, build a chord by writing the 1st, 3rd, and 5th notes of the **E Major** scale.
    Write and circle the chord notes on the above keyboard.
    The notes of the **E Major** chord are: _____, _____, _____.

5. Write the chords in both clefs. Notice which chord uses line notes
    and which chord uses space notes.

    L.H.   R.H.

    E Major chords

    E Major key signature

6. What black keys are used in the **E Major** scale? _____, _____, _____, _____.

7. Play and say the **E Major** scale and chord. Memorize which sharps are used
    and notice how they are written in the above key signature.

The chord built on the 1st note of the scale is called the **tonic** chord ($\underline{\text{I}}$)	The chord built on the 5th note of the scale is called the **dominant** chord ($\underline{\text{V}}$)

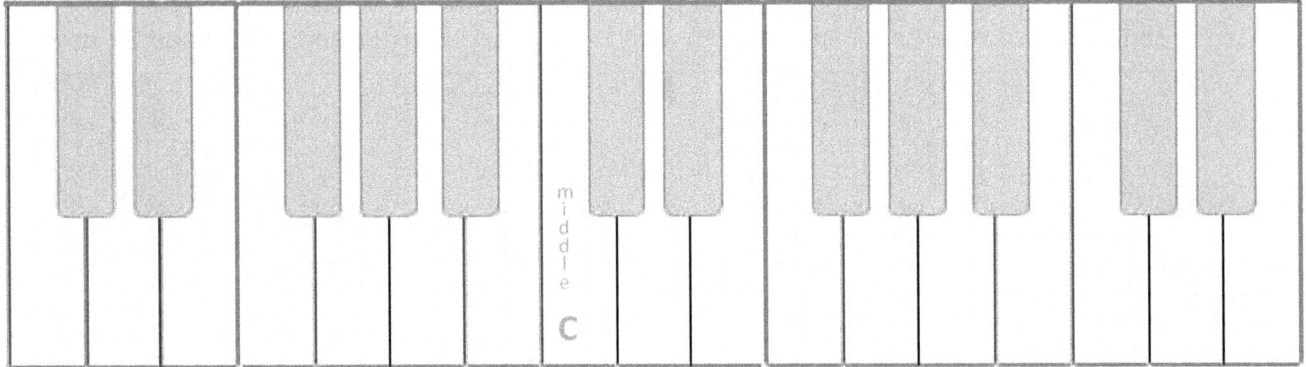

middle C

tonic chord + dominant chord + tonic chord = authentic cadence

Chord-name*:

$\underline{\text{I}}$	$\underline{\text{V}}$	$\underline{\text{I}}$		$\underline{\text{I}}$	$\underline{\text{V}}$	$\underline{\text{I}}$
tonic	dominant	tonic		tonic	dominant	tonic

When you write major scales or chords, ALWAYS use capital letters.

Keyboard Activities

1. Write the notes of the **E Major** position for the left hand. Circle the 1st and 5th notes.

2. Play a chord on the 1st note and a chord on the 5th note. Then, write them on the keys and staff above. These are the MOST important chords in the key of **E Major**.

3. Highlight the dominant chord on the keyboard starting on the 5th note of **E Major.**

4. The tonic note is _____ and its chord is on the _____ degree of the scale.
   The dominant note is _____ and its chord is on the _____ degree of the scale.

5. Hands alone, play back and forth between the tonic and dominant chords, then try playing them with both hands together.

6. If you play a chord on every note of the **E Major** scale, how many chords are using any of the black keys F♯, C♯, G♯, and D♯?_____

Building the Parallel E Minor 5-Note Scale

Major: W-W-H - W

major tetrachord

Minor: W-H-W - W

minor tetrachord

The **major** 5-note scale has a half-step between the 3rd and 4th notes.

The **minor** 5-note scale has a half-step between the 2nd and 3rd notes.
(Move your 3rd finger down a half-step)

E Major

F# G#

E   A   B

Scale degree:

W or H pattern:

e minor

Scale degree:

W or H pattern:

1. On the left keyboard, write the scale degrees and W or H for the **E Major** 5-note scale.

2. Play the **E Major** pattern, but now lower the 3rd note by a half-step to create a half-step between the 2nd and 3rd notes.

3. What kind of accidental is used? _____ Name the lowered note: _____

4. Write the new **e minor** 5-note scale on the right keyboard. _____, _____, _____, _____, _____. (*ALWAYS use smaller lowercase letters for minor*).

5. What finger changes position? _____ Mark or color the half-steps on the keyboards above. The half-step in the 5-note **e minor** scale is between the notes _____ and _____. Notice where the half-step is between the major and minor tetrachords and how it changes the 5-note scales.

Keyboard Activities

6. This minor 5-note scale uses _____ white key(s) and _____ black key(s).

7. Which fingers play the G-natural in both hands? LH:_____ RH: _____

Building the E Minor Chord

(Left Hand)

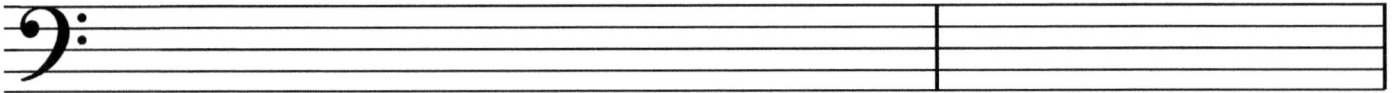

Note-name:

Finger-number:

e minor chord

(Right Hand)

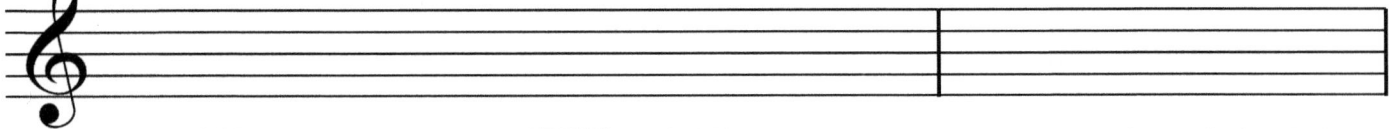

Note-name:

Finger-number:

e minor chord

1. Write the **e minor** pentascale (5-note scale) in both clefs and add any accidentals.

2. Write the note-names and the finger-numbers below the name of the notes.

3. Circle the two fingers and note-names with the half-step in each hand.

4. On the staff, highlight the 1st, 3rd, and 5th notes and write the chord on the staff. The notes of the **e minor** chord are: _____, _____, _____. Do you remember what other major key is related to the **e minor** chord? _____ Major.

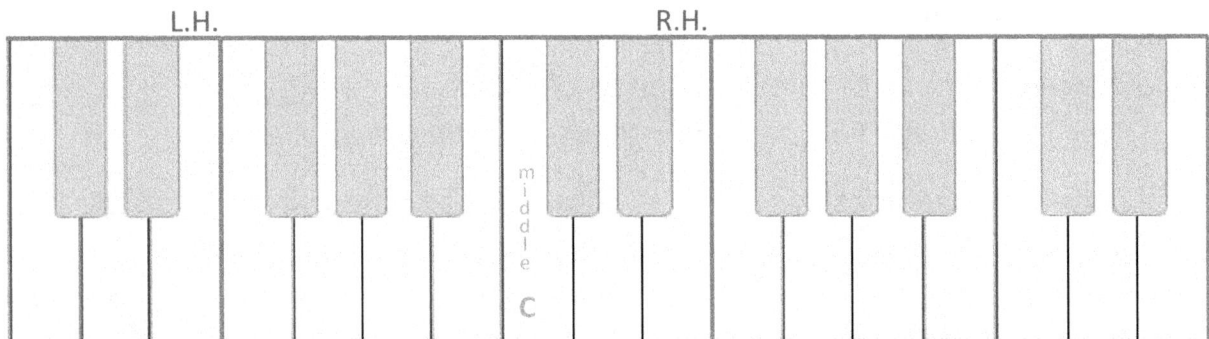

5. Write and highlight the notes of the **e minor** chord on the keyboard above.

6. While at your own keyboard, practice switching from **e minor** to **E Major**. Notice how your hand position changes as you move the 3rd finger from the g♮ to the G♯.

How we build it: **W-H-W + W-H-W + W** = natural minor scale

🎹 **Keyboard Activities**

Looking at the **E Major** scale and key signature (see page 35), do the following:

1. What is the 6th note of the **E Major** scale? _____. Highlight the note on the left keyboard below.

2. Using the same notes and accidentals, play a scale on the 6th note of the **E Major** scale to make *the relative natural minor scale of E Major*. Notice it uses the same notes and keys as **E Major**, but begins and ends on the note C♯ (the 6th note of **E Major**).

3. The **E Major** and **c♯ minor** scales use _____ white key(s) and _____ black key(s). They are *relative scales* because they contain the same notes and use the same key signature.

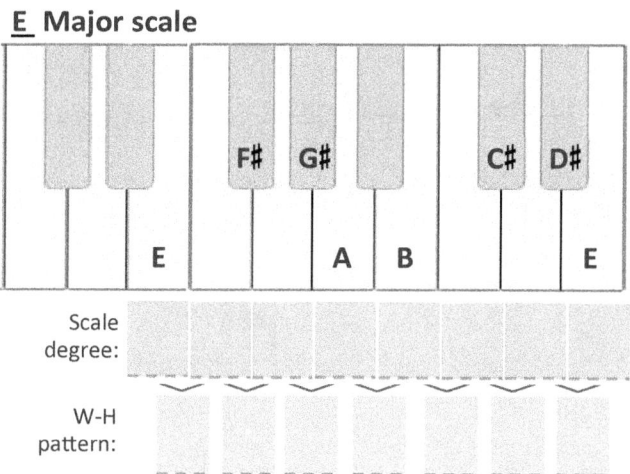

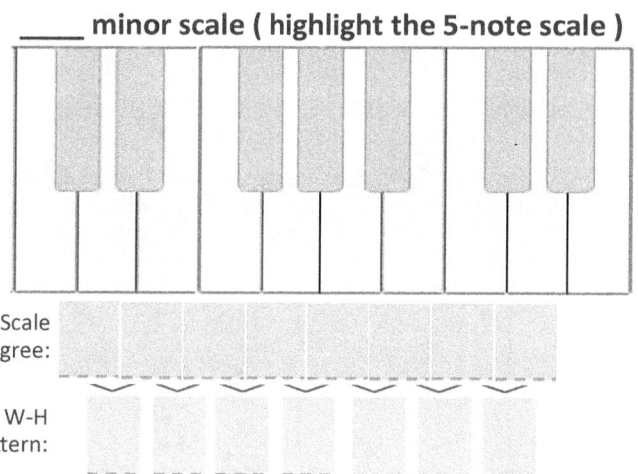

E Major scale

F♯ G♯   C♯ D♯

E   A B   E

Scale degree:

W-H pattern:

_____ **minor scale (highlight the 5-note scale)**

Scale degree:

W-H pattern:

4. Using the same notes as **E Major**, but starting on the note C♯, write the scale on the keyboard diagram. Highlight the new 5-note **c♯ minor** scale.
   The notes are: _____, _____, _____, _____, _____.

5. How many sharps does **c♯ minor** have? _____
   Circle and name the sharps: _____, _____, _____, _____.

6. Circle the scale degrees and keyboard notes where the half-steps are in both of these relative scales. Notice how they are different. The half-steps in the **c♯ natural minor** scale are between the scale degrees: _____ & _____, and _____ & _____; and between the notes: _____ & _____, and _____ & _____.

Building the C♯ Minor Chord

1. Write the **c♯ minor** pentascale (5-note scale) in both clefs and add any accidentals.

2. Write the finger-numbers and note-names below the staff. Circle the 1ˢᵗ, 3ʳᵈ, and 5ᵗʰ fingerings and note-names in each hand.

3. Circle and highlight the 1ˢᵗ, 3ʳᵈ, and 5ᵗʰ notes and write the chord on the staff. The notes of the **c♯ minor** chord are: _____, _____, _____.

(Left Hand)   (Right Hand)

Finger-number: c♯ min chord   c♯ min chord

Note-names:

4. Highlight and write the notes of the **c♯ minor** chord on the keyboard below.

5. How many half-steps are between the note C♯ and the note E? _____

6. How many half-steps are between the note E and the note G♯? _____

7. What notes are shared in the **E Major** and **c♯ minor** chord? _____ & _____

m
i
d
d
l
e
C

Remember the accidentals!

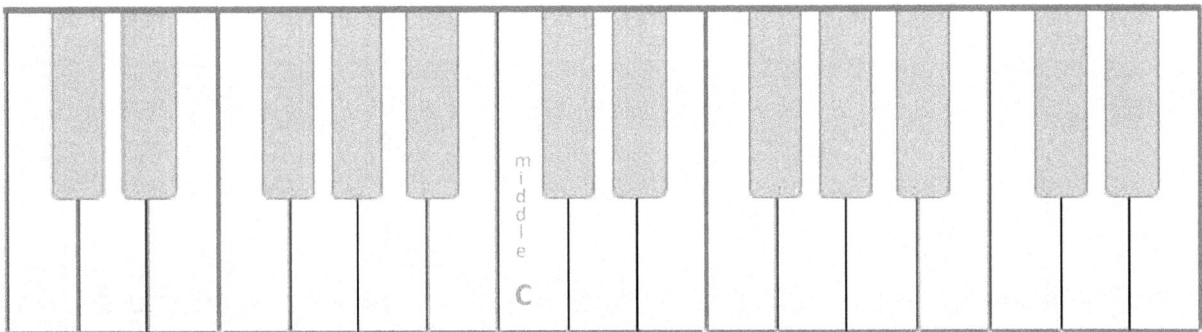

Challenge Activities

Building chords on the **E Major** scale, remember F♯, C♯, G♯, D♯ (Circle the correct answer).

8. Play a chord on the 2ⁿᵈ note of **E Major**. Is it major or minor?

9. Play a chord on the 3ʳᵈ note of **E Major**. Is it major or minor?

10. Play a chord on the 4ᵗʰ note of **E Major**. Is it major or minor?

11. Play a chord on the 5ᵗʰ note of **E Major**. Is it major or minor?

Major Tetrachord + Whole-Step
(W - W - H)   +   (W)

1. Write the **F Major** pentascale (5-note scale) in both clefs and add any accidentals. (Write the major note names in capital letters.)

2. Mark the half-steps and the whole-steps on the second line.

3. Write the finger-numbers. Circle the fingerings and note-names with half-steps in each hand, and on the staff.

4. Highlight the 1ˢᵗ, 3ʳᵈ, and 5ᵗʰ notes on each staff.

(Left Hand)

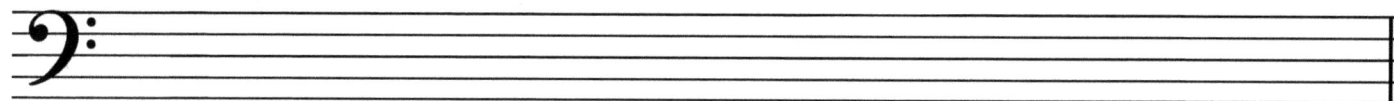

Note-name:

W-H pattern:

Finger-number:

(Right Hand)

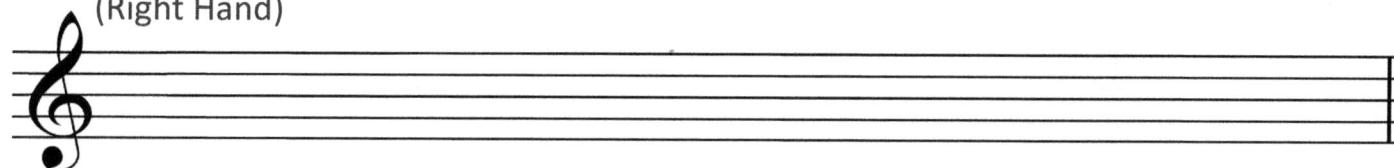

Note-name:

W-H pattern:

Finger-number:

▐▐▐ Keyboard Activities

5. Play your **F Major** 5-note scale up and down, using staccato notes.

6. Play your 5-note scale with half notes and then with quarter notes.

7. This 5-note scale uses _____ white keys and the black key _____.

Learning F Major Hand Position

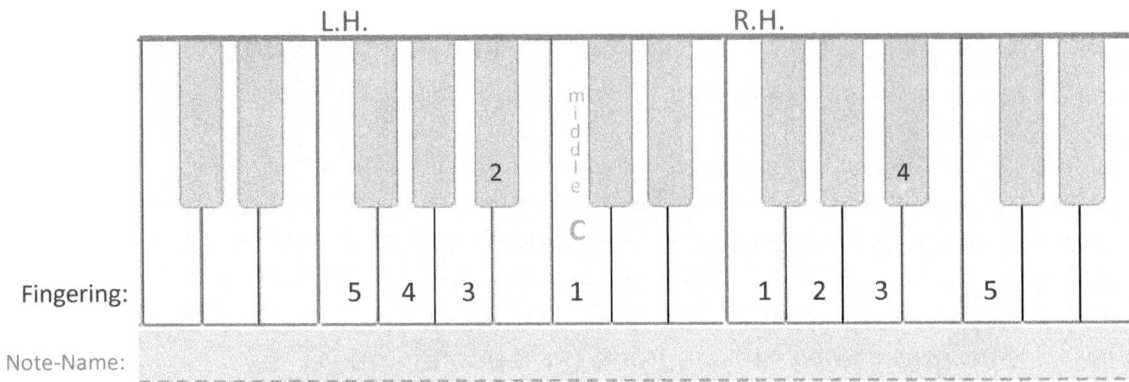

L.H.　　　　　　　　　　　R.H.

Fingering:　　　　5　4　3　　1　　　1　2　3　　5

Note-Name:

1. Write each note of the **F Major** position below the keyboard diagram.

2. Highlight the **F Major** pentascale above and below middle C.

3. Circle the note-names and fingerings of the half-step in each hand.

4. The half-step is between the notes _____ and _____. This hand position stretches from the notes _____ to _____.

L.H.　　　　　　　　　　　R.H.

Scale degree:

5. Color the **F Major** position for both hands.

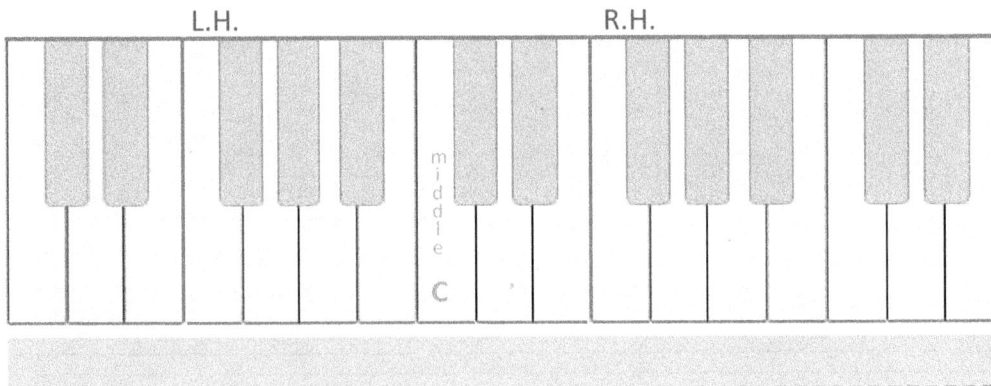

6. Write and circle the note-names of the 1st, 3rd, and 5th degrees on the keyboard for both hands. This is the **F Major** chord.

7. How many white keys between your two hand positions? ____

8. This chord uses _____ white key(s) and _____ black key(s).

▯▯▯ Keyboard Activities

9. Play a chord on every note of the **F Major** pentascale. Remember the B♭.

10. How many half-steps between the notes F and A? _____ And between A and C? _____

Building the 8-Note F Major Scale

F Major
Scale

Major Scale: 2 Major Tetrachords Connected with a Whole-Step

This is how we build it: W-W-H + W + W-W-H = major scale

tetrachord   tetrachord

Hint: Be sure to keep a half-step between the 3rd and 4th notes and the 7th and 8th notes.

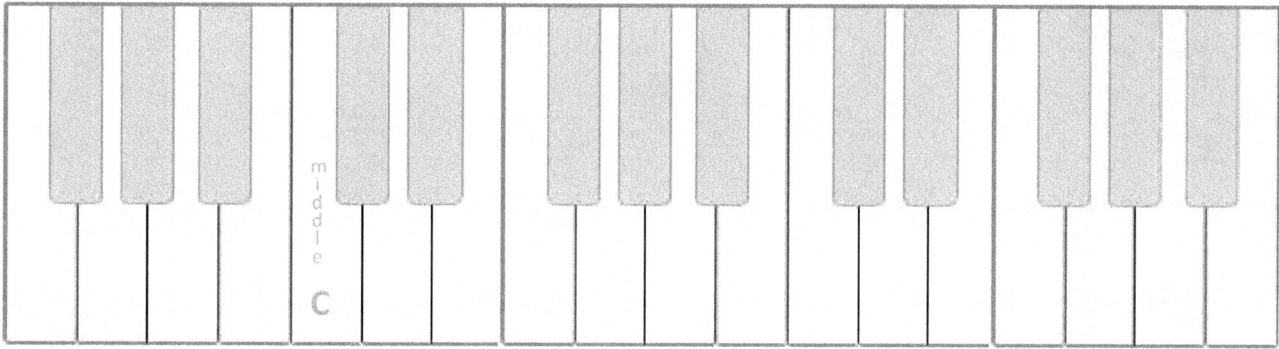

Scale degree:

W-H pattern

chord notes

1. Start below middle C. Using the above formula, write each note from **F** to **F**.

2. Write the scale degrees. Identify the whole-steps (W) and the half-steps (H).

3. Color the half-steps in each tetrachord. They are: _____ to_____ and _____ to _____.
   What whole-step connects the two tetrachords? ____ to ____.

4. Above middle C, build a chord by writing the 1st, 3rd, and 5th notes of the **F Major** scale.
   Write and circle the chord notes on the above keyboard.
   The notes of the **F Major** chord are: _____, _____, _____.

5. Write the chords in both clefs. Notice which chord uses line notes
   and which chord uses space notes.

   L.H.   R.H.

   F Major chords

   F Major key signature

6. What black key is used in the **F Major** scale? _____.

7. Play and say the **F Major** scale and chord. Memorize which flat is used and
   notice how it is written in the above key signature.

Writing Essentials for the Beginner Pianist Copyright © 2014 Clara Castano & Catherine A. Thompson   43

The chord built on the 1st note of the scale is called the **tonic** chord (I̅)

The chord built on the 5th note of the scale is called the **dominant** chord (V̅)

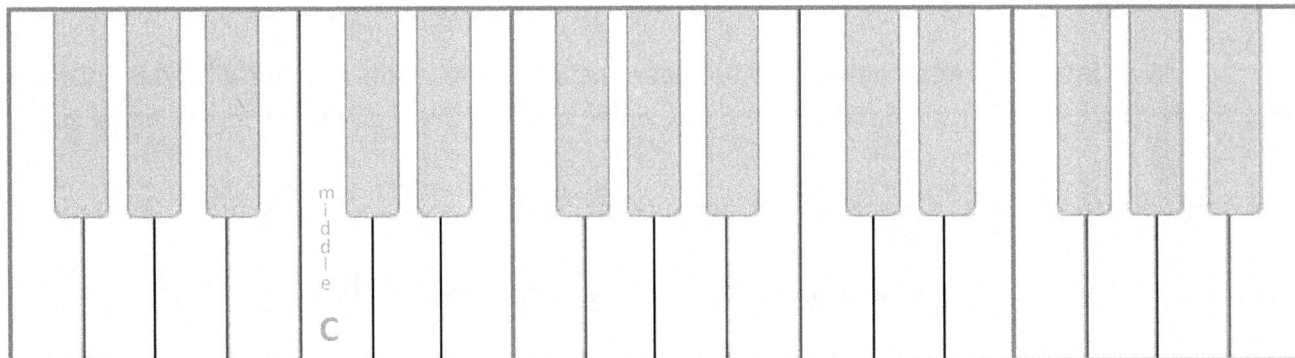

tonic chord **+** dominant chord **+** tonic chord **=** authentic cadence

Chord-name*:
tonic dominant tonic   tonic dominant tonic

When you write major scales or chords, ALWAYS use capital letters.

🎹 Keyboard Activities

1. Write the notes of the **F Major** position for the left hand. Circle the 1st and 5th notes.

2. Play a chord on the 1st note and a chord on the 5th note. Then, write them on the keys and staff above. These are the MOST important chords in the key of **F Major**.

3. Highlight the dominant chord on the keyboard starting on the 5th note of **F Major**.

4. The tonic note is _____ and its chord is on the _____ degree of the scale.
   The dominant note is _____ and its chord is on the _____ degree of the scale.

5. Hands alone, play back and forth between the tonic and dominant chords, then try playing them with both hands together.

6. If you play a chord on every note of the **F Major** scale, how many chords are using the black key B♭? _____

Building the Parallel F Minor 5-Note Scale

Major: W-W-H - W
major tetrachord

Minor: W-H-W - W
minor tetrachord

The **major** 5-note scale has a half-step between the 3rd and 4th notes.

The **minor** 5-note scale has a half-step between the 2nd and 3rd notes.
(Move your 3rd finger down a half-step)

F Major

Bb

F G A♮ C

Scale degree:

W-H pattern:

f minor

Scale degree:

W-H pattern:

1. On the left keyboard, write the scale degrees and W or H for the **F Major** 5-note scale.

2. Play the **F Major** pattern, but now lower the 3rd note by a half-step to create a half-step between the 2nd and 3rd notes.

3. What kind of accidental is used? _____ Name the lowered note: _____

4. Write the new **f minor** 5-note scale on the right keyboard. _____, _____, _____, _____, _____. (*ALWAYS use smaller lowercase letters for minor*).

5. What finger changes position? _____ Mark or color the half-steps on the keyboards above. The half-step in the 5-note **f minor** scale is between the notes _____ and _____. Notice where the half-step is between the major and minor tetrachords and how it changes the 5-note scales.

Keyboard Activities

6. This minor 5-note scale uses _____ white key(s) and _____ black key(s).

7. Which fingers play the A-flat in both hands? LH:_____ RH: _____

(Left Hand)

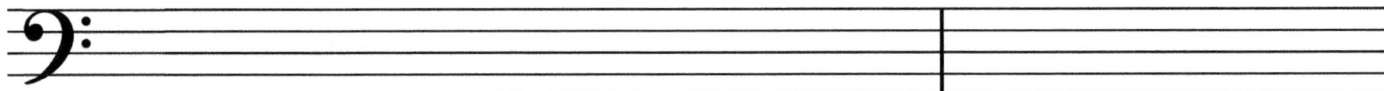

Note-name:

Finger-number:

f minor chord

(Right Hand)

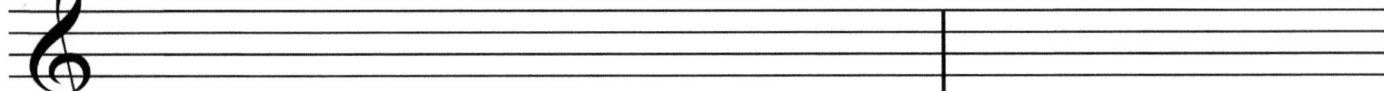

Note-name:

Finger-number:

f minor chord

1. Write the **f minor** pentascale (5-note scale) in both clefs and add any accidentals.

2. Write the note-names and the finger-numbers below the name of the notes.

3. Circle the two fingers and note-names with the half-step in each hand.

4. On the staff, highlight the 1st, 3rd, and 5th notes and write the chord on the staff. The notes of the **f minor** chord are: _____, _____, _____.

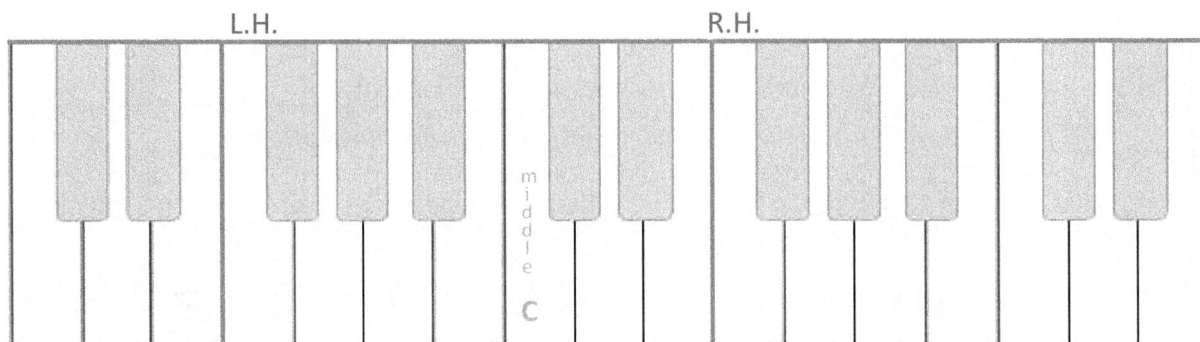

L.H.   R.H.

middle C

5. Write and highlight the notes of the **f minor** chord on the keyboard above.

6. While at your own keyboard, practice switching from **f minor** to **F Major**. Notice how your hand position changes as you move the 3rd finger from the a♭ to the A♮.

> How we build it: **W-H-W + W-H-W + W** = natural minor scale

Looking at the **F Major** scale and key signature (see page 43), do the following:

1. What is the 6th note of the **F Major** scale? _____. Highlight the note on the left keyboard below.

2. Using the same notes and accidentals, play a scale on the 6th note of the **F Major** scale to make *the relative natural minor scale of F Major*. Notice it uses the same notes and keys as **F Major**, but begins and ends on the note D (the 6th note of **F Major**).

3. The **F Major** and **d minor** scales use _____ white key(s) and _____ black key(s). They are *relative scales* because they contain the same notes and use the same key signature.

F Major scale

Bb

| F | G | A | | C | D | E | F |

Scale degree:

W-H pattern:

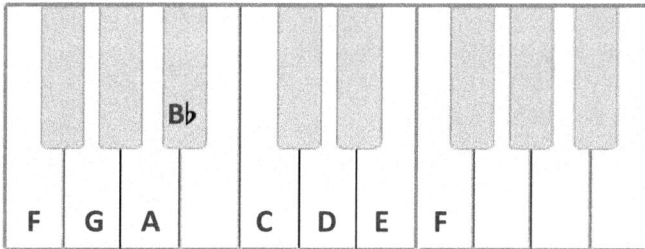

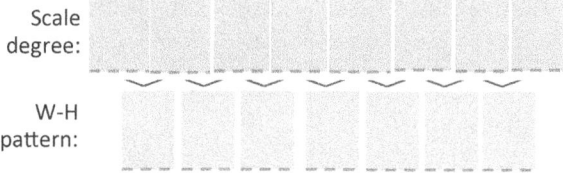

_____ minor scale (highlight the 5-note scale)

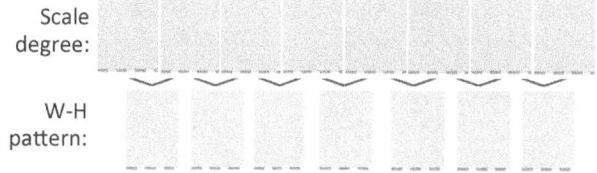

Scale degree:

W-H pattern:

4. Using the same notes as **F Major**, but starting on the note D, write the scale on the keyboard diagram. Highlight the new 5-note **d minor** scale.
The notes are: _____, _____, _____, _____, _____.

5. How many flats does **d minor** have? _____ Circle and name the flat: _____.

6. Circle the scale degrees and keyboard notes where the half-steps are in both of these relative scales. Notice how they are different. The half-steps in the **d natural minor** scale are between the scale degrees: _____ & _____, and _____ & _____; and between the notes: _____ & _____, and _____ & _____.

Building the D Minor Chord

1. Write the **d minor** pentascale (5-note scale) in both clefs and add any accidentals.

2. Write the finger-numbers and note-names below the staff. Circle the 1st, 3rd, and 5th fingerings and note-names in each hand.

3. Circle and highlight the 1st, 3rd, and 5th notes and write the chord on the staff. The notes of the **d minor** chord are: _____, _____, _____.

(Left Hand)   (Right Hand)

Finger-number: _____   d min chord   _____   d min chord

Note-names: _____   _____

4. Highlight and write the notes of the **d minor** chord on the keyboard below.

5. How many half-steps are between the note D and the note F? _____

6. How many half-steps are between the note F and the note A? _____

7. What notes are shared in the **F Major** and **d minor** chord? _____ & _____

middle C

Remember the accidental!

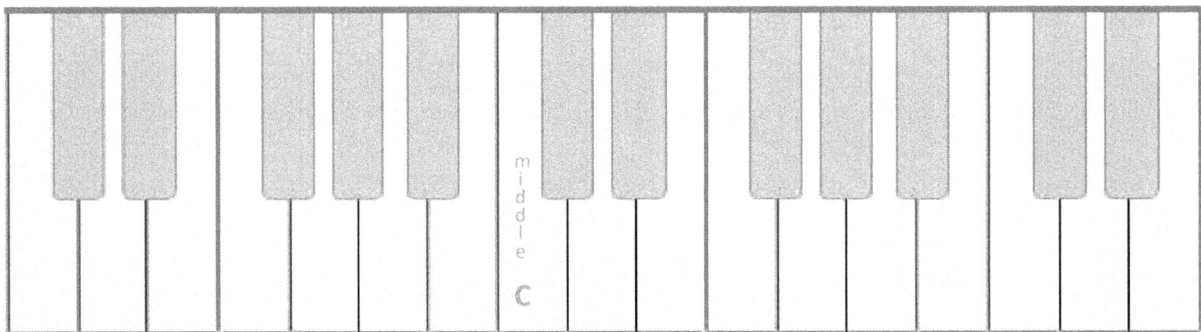

Challenge Activities

Building chords on the **F Major** scale notes. Remember the B♭. (Circle the correct answer)

8. Play a chord on the 2nd note of **F Major**. Is it major or minor?

9. Play a chord on the 3rd note of **F Major**. Is it major or minor?

10. Play a chord on the 4th note of **F Major**. Is it major or minor?

11. Play a chord on the 5th note of **F Major**. Is it major or minor?

Summary Test Exercises

5-note Scales, Major Scales, and Major & Minor Chords

A. Match each 5-note scale to its name.

1. ____   a. C Major

2. ____   b. c minor

3. ____   c. F Major

4. ____   d. f minor

5. ____   e. G Major

6. ____   f. g minor

7. ____   g. D Major

8. ____   h. d minor

9. ____   i. A Major

10. ____   j. a minor

11. ____   k. E Major

12. ____   l. e minor

A. Add the correct sharp(s) or flat(s) to make these major scales. Write any accidentals in the key signature.

1. C Major

    key signature

2. G Major

3. D Major

4. F Major

B. Add the correct sharp(s) or flat(s) to make these major scales. Write any accidentals in the key signature.

1. C Major

    key signature

2. G Major

3. D Major

4. F Major

A. Use the correct accidentals (♯ ♭ ♮) to build the major and minor chords.

Remember to use uppercase capital letters when writing the names of the major chords and lowercase letters for the minor chords.

1.

Chord name: _____ Major _____ minor _____ Major _____ minor _____ Major _____ minor

2.

Chord name: _____ Major _____ minor _____ Major _____ minor _____ Major _____ minor

B. Use the correct accidentals (♯ ♭ ♮) to build the major and minor chords.

Remember to use uppercase capital letters when writing the names of the major chords and lowercase letters for the minor chords

1.

Chord name: _____ Major _____ minor _____ Major _____ minor _____ Major _____ minor

2.

Chord name: _____ Major _____ minor _____ Major _____ minor _____ Major _____ minor

Piano Technique Supplement with Fingerings

- Helpful Suggestions.

- Major and Parallel Minor 5-Note scales.

- Major and Relative Natural Minor Scales.

- Authentic Root Position Cadences are included with all Major Scales.

HELPFUL SUGGESTIONS FOR USING THE TECHNICAL SUPPLEMENT FOR BUILDING EARLY LEVEL PIANO TECHNIQUE

1. Complete a particular written assignment before practicing the matching piano pattern.

2. Be sure to do the assigned keyboard activities in each chapter so that you understand the pattern you are learning. Exercises maybe be played with *legato or staccato or with other rhythms as suggested by the teacher: as well as repeated in other registers of the piano.*

3. The 5-note patterns may be practiced at whatever speed feels best. Be sure to achieve an evenness between the fingers and the hand weight on the keys. Follow the recommendations of your teacher for developing your hand position: such as how you hold your hand above the keys, drop and lift motions of the wrist, including the effort to prevent your bottom knuckles from buckling. Be sure to keep your fingers curved. Play on the very tips of your fingers, and NOT on the back of your fingertips with straight fingers.

4. Teachers may wish to have very young or less coordinated students use the tetrachord style scale fingerings for the 8-note major and minor scales. This method allows, especially young players to learn their accidentals and scales before they are ready for the "cross-under" gesture of playing with one hand or hands together. It is also a great way for any beginner pianist to experiment with the different locations of keyboard geography; and will increase their confidence with hand placement on the black keys.

   tetrachord fingerings: Place the Left Hand 5th finger on the tonic (starting note) and the 5th finger of the Right Hand on the octave above. Without using the thumbs, place the remaining fingers on the notes. Notice that both 2nd fingers will be next to each other:

   L.H. 5-4-3-2   R.H. 2-3-4-5

   Using this method will make it easier and less challenging for beginners to get comfortable exploring hand positions and major and minor keys. When they are ready to play with one octave scales with one hand, or both, they will already have learned the notes and key signatures; creating an easier transition. The technical supplement includes the fingerings to help with this transition.

5. Avoid rushing through the exercises. Like any athlete, you must work on your form. All of your future technique is built on learning these early level hand movements to develop strength, coordination and ease of movement.

6. The exercises may be learned in any order, but we suggest learning the major 5-note patterns first, then follow them with either the parallel minor 5-note pattern or the 8-note major scale, followed by the authentic cadence. The relative natural minors have been included as an option of exploration for students who exhibit accelerated learning or methods that encourage discovery of key relationships.

5-Note Scale Fingerings & Authentic Cadences
C Major, C Parallel Minor, and A Relative Minor

For early note reading an effort has been made to keep the notes on the staff as much as possible, therefore some of the hand positions are notated two octaves apart. You are given the choice to follow the suggestions to adjust either hand up or down an octave.

C Major

c natural minor (parallel)

a natural minor (relative)

8-Note Scale Fingerings & Authentic Cadences
C Major, C Parallel Minor, and A Relative Minor

For early note reading an effort has been made to keep the notes on the staff as much as possible, therefore some of the hand positions are notated two octaves apart. You are given the choice to follow the suggestions to adjust either hand up or down an octave.

C Major

c natural minor (parallel)

a natural minor (relative)

5-Note Scale Fingerings & Authentic Cadences
G Major, G Parallel Minor, and E Relative Minor

For early note reading an effort has been made to keep the notes on the staff as much as possible, therefore some of the hand positions are notated two octaves apart. You are given the choice to follow the suggestions to adjust either hand up or down an octave.

G Major

g natural minor (parallel)

e natural minor (relative)

8-Note Scale Fingerings & Authentic Cadences
G Major, G Parallel Minor, and E Relative Minor

For early note reading an effort has been made to keep the notes on the staff as much as possible, therefore some of the hand positions are notated two octaves apart. You are given the choice to follow the suggestions to adjust either hand up or down an octave.

G Major

g natural minor (parallel)

e natural minor (relative)

5-Note Scale Fingerings & Authentic Cadences
D Major, D Parallel Minor, and B Relative Minor

For early note reading an effort has been made to keep the notes on the staff as much as possible, therefore some of the hand positions are notated two octaves apart. You are given the choice to follow the suggestions to adjust either hand up or down an octave.

D Major

d natural minor (parallel)

b natural minor (relative)

8-Note Scale Fingerings & Authentic Cadences
D Major, D Parallel Minor, and B Relative Minor

For early note reading an effort has been made to keep the notes on the staff as much as possible, therefore some of the hand positions are notated two octaves apart. You are given the choice to follow the suggestions to adjust either hand up or down an octave.

D Major

d natural minor (parallel)

b natural minor (relative)

* Check with your teacher for their preferred fingering for the **b natural** minor scale.

5-Note Scale Fingerings & Authentic Cadences
A Major, A Parallel Minor, and F♯ Relative Minor

For early note reading an effort has been made to keep the notes on the staff as much as possible, therefore some of the hand positions are notated two octaves apart. You are given the choice to follow the suggestions to adjust either hand up or down an octave.

A Major

Play left hand an octave higher

a natural minor (parallel)

Play left hand an octave higher

f♯ natural minor (relative)

8-Note Scale Fingerings & Authentic Cadences
A Major, A Parallel Minor, and F♯ Relative Minor

For early note reading an effort has been made to keep the notes on the staff as much as possible, therefore some of the hand positions are notated two octaves apart. You are given the choice to follow the suggestions to adjust either hand up or down an octave.

A Major

a natural minor (parallel)

f♯ natural minor (relative)

* Check with your teacher for their preferred fingering for the **f♯ natural** minor scale.

5-Note Scale Fingerings & Authentic Cadences
E Major, E Parallel Minor, and C♯ Relative Minor

For early note reading an effort has been made to keep the notes on the staff as much as possible, therefore some of the hand positions are notated two octaves apart. You are given the choice to follow the suggestions to adjust either hand up or down an octave.

E Major

e natural minor (parallel)

c♯ natural minor (relative)

8-Note Scale Fingerings & Authentic Cadences
E Major, E Parallel Minor, and C♯ Relative Minor

For early note reading an effort has been made to keep the notes on the staff as much as possible, therefore some of the hand positions are notated two octaves apart. You are given the choice to follow the suggestions to adjust either hand up or down an octave.

E Major

e natural minor (parallel)

c♯ natural minor (relative)

* Check with your teacher for their preferred fingering for the **C♯ natural** minor scale.

5-Note Scale Fingerings & Authentic Cadences
F Major, F Parallel Minor, and D Relative Minor

For early note reading an effort has been made to keep the notes on the staff as much as possible, therefore some of the hand positions are notated two octaves apart. You are given the choice to follow the suggestions to adjust either hand up or down an octave.

F Major

F natural minor (parallel)

d natural minor (relative)

8-Note Scale Fingerings & Authentic Cadences
F Major, F Parallel Minor, and D Relative Minor

For early note reading an effort has been made to keep the notes on the staff as much as possible, therefore some of the hand positions are notated two octaves apart. You are given the choice to follow the suggestions to adjust either hand up or down an octave.

F Major

f natural minor (parallel)

Play left hand an octave higher

d natural minor (relative)